Fi

E Shaw

BIBLIOBAZAAR

FIRE SURVEYS

OR,

A SUMMARY OF THE PRINCIPLES TO BE OBSERVED

IN

ESTIMATING THE RISK OF BUILDINGS.

BY

E. M. SHAW,

LONDON FIRE BRIGADE.

LONDON:
EFFINGHAM WILSON, ROYAL EXCHANGE.
1872.

INTRODUCTION.

The subject of safety or danger from fire is one which appears to present itself in different forms to various minds according to the point of view from which it is approached, and the amount of practical knowledge of sound principles brought to bear on it.

Why this should be so it is not for me to say, or even to suggest; but the fact itself is quite beyond doubt, in corroboration of which I venture to assert that there exist buildings which are said by their owners, occupiers, insurers, or others interested, to be the very models of all that is secure and excellent, and which are at the same time cited by those whose business lies in the direction of obviating or reducing the physical consequences of disasters by fire, as dangerous in the extreme, indeed in certain instances so liable to rapid destruction as to constitute a special subject of instruction to those learning the business, being the most complete examples which are known, very nearly the most complete which can be imagined, of a combination of all or many of the greatest and most acknowledged dangers.

It certainly seems most strange that on such a subject views so diametrically opposite should be held, on the one hand by owners of property or those interested in the pecuniary consequences of disasters by fire, and on the other by those professionally engaged in the practical work of reducing damages.

The object of the following pages is to make, in summary, an exposition of views which I have long held and taught to those who serve with me, and which have formed the basis of all the recommendations and advice which I have given concerning the general subject of safety or danger from fire in England, in the colonies, and in foreign countries for many years.

E. M. SHAW.

ARRANGEMENT OF THE SEVERAL BRANCHES OF THE SUBJECT.

In making an inspection of a building for the purpose of ascertaining its condition with regard to danger from fire, the following points should be specially and separately considered:—

FIRE SURVEYS.

1. General Description.

In order to make a complete survey of a building it is advisable to obtain a plan, an elevation, and some sections.

The first point for consideration is the general description of the premises, as, for instance, whether they consist of one or more buildings, and whether the several parts wholly or partially communicate with each other; also whether they are used as a private dwelling, lodging, hotel, club, church, theatre, warehouse, factory, or otherwise. It should also be noted whether the premises are old or new, and whether they have been altered since their first construction, or are still used for the same purposes for which they were originally intended. Buildings not originally constructed for carrying heavy weights or machinery, and afterwards adapted for these purposes, are seldom very safe; and buildings which have undergone much structural alteration are almost invariably unsafe. There are, of course, very many and important exceptions to these general rules, and, in making an inspection of a building, these exceptions should be specially noted; but, where they do not exist or cannot be easily discovered, it may generally be assumed

General description. Buildings, number of. Communication. Business. Age of premises. Alterations. Adaptation. Structural alteration. Exceptions.

that the soundness of the structure is at least doubtful.

Throughout a survey it is well to bear in mind the following remarks, which may tend to prevent illusions or confusion of ideas concerning a subject simple enough in itself, but very much misunderstood by those who have not studied it, and almost always misrepresented by ignorant or interested persons.

Concerning so-called fire-proof buildings.

Use of the term fire-proof.

So little attention appears to have been paid to the real meaning of the term fire-proof, that it seems necessary, notwithstanding the repeated practical warnings which great calamities by fire have given during the last quarter of a century in all parts of the world, to endeavour to impress on those interested the incontrovertible fact that, in treating of fireproof structures, distinct reference should be made not only to the style, material, and capacity of the building itself, but also, and in a much greater degree, to the nature, quantity, and classification of its contents. These points are inextricably mixed up together, and no amount of legislation can separate them; on the contrary, there is abundant evidence to show that much evil has been done by the ordinary use of the expression fire-proof, which is commonly applied to the structure alone, thus utterly ignoring the obvious fact that, with regard to risk of fire, the contents of a building are of much greater importance than the building itself. Thus, a building, which would be perfectly fireproof as an office or private dwelling-house, might be most dangerous if converted into a factory or warehouse. It may be laid down as a rule

Caution about use of the term fire-proof.

that a building, to be truly fireproof, should be divided into compartments, and so constructed that the contents of any one compartment might be consumed by fire, without calcining, melting, or otherwise destroying the surrounding horizontal and upright partitions, and therefore without communicating fire to the other rooms or floors.

In such a building, even without the attendance of firemen and engines, no fire could destroy a greater quantity of property than the contents of one compartment; but the probability is that in every case the firemen would be enabled to realise a sufficiently large salvage to repay any additional outlay attending the improved construction.

There is in this country the greatest reluctance to any legislation which may appear, however remotely, to fetter or otherwise interfere with the free course of trade, but a reference to the Building Acts, 14 Geo. 3, cap. 78; 7 and 8 Vic., cap. 84; 18 and 19 Vic., cap. 120 and 122; the Gunpowder Act, 23 and 24 Vic., cap. 139; the Petroleum Act, 25 and 26 Vic., cap. 66, and many others, will suffice to show that there is a point at which it has always been acknowledged as a duty of the legislature to interfere for the general welfare, and, however inconvenient any change might for the moment prove, it can hardly be denied that the ultimate results of a compulsory subdivision of risks and classification of goods would be most beneficial to all large mercantile cities. Until this is done it is not too much to say that there is serious danger and no possible advantage in giving legislative or any other sanction to the use of the vague term fire-proof, which has been applied indiscriminately to all sorts of buildings even where arches are carried on iron girders, or held together by iron ties, notwithstanding the obvious fact that no structure can be properly called fire-proof, the ultimate strength of which depends on any metal.

---

2. Site.

Building, position of. Nature of ground, whether flat or hilly. Approaches, nature of. Approaches, sufficiency of. Approaches, freedom of.

The next point for consideration is whether a building is situated on level ground or on a hill, and whether the adjoining land is level, hilly, or undulating; also whether the approaches are by roads, streets, walks, fields, gardens, or otherwise, and whether they are sufficient for the purpose, and likely to be at all times available. It very rarely happens that any conclusion can be formed concerning the safety or danger of a building from a consideration of its site alone, but this subject considered in connection with several others which follow may frequently be of very great and occasionally of paramount importance. Thus, for instance, if a dwelling-house were placed on the top of a precipitous hill, it might happen that, although abundant help in the way of firemen and fire-engines might be in close proximity, the house might, notwithstanding this, be practically beyond the reach of assistance in the event of a fire occurring. Again, if a large factory or heavily-stocked warehouse were situated in a very narrow street, it might happen that only one engine could be brought near enough to work upon it. The whole of the site of the premises, therefore, and of all the surroundings and approaches, should be carefully studied before any opinion is formed as to their safety or danger.

The distance apart of buildings fronting each other should be in proportion to their height; in fact, as a simple rule, it might be laid down that they should be separated by a distance equal to half their combined height. Thus, for instance, a building of 60 feet and a building of 30 feet high might safely occupy opposite sides of a street 45 feet wide. Buildings, distance apart of.

---

3. Foundation.

The safety of a building depends very considerably on the foundations. If these are thoroughly sound and good there is no probability of unequal settlements and consequent cracks or fractures of the walls. It may be assumed that every building not founded on a rock is always undergoing a depression or sinking downwards, even after it has been in existence for years or centuries; but, as long as this settlement takes place all over the structure, and equally in all parts, no injury is likely to happen. When, however, a building settles down considerably in some parts and only slightly in others, or when it settles down perhaps slightly in some parts and not at all in others, then serious danger of fractured walls may be apprehended. In making a survey of a building it must be remembered that a settlement may take place in the masonry or other structural work as well as in the foundation, and it is most important to observe whether trifling inequalities of settlement which may be discovered arise from imperfections in the work itself, or shocks subsequent to its completion, or may be attributed to natural defects in the site. In the former case the fractures may be repaired, the

Foundation, soundness of.

Foundation, settlement of.

Foundation, equal settlement of.

Foundation, unequal settlement of.

Masonry, settlement in.

Masonry, defect in, danger of.

walls may be strengthened by supports, buttresses, ties, and a variety of contrivances, but in the latter it is hardly too much to say that it is almost impossible to obviate the danger. In a certain sense there is no such thing as a bad natural foundation. That is to say, any person of experience after examining a site ought to be able to state absolutely whether it is fit to carry a building or not, and, if it is fit, ought to be able to say what class and weight of building might be erected on it. In speaking, therefore, of natural defects in a site, nothing more is intended to be conveyed than that a site in its natural state is unable to carry in a satisfactory manner certain buildings which have been erected upon it, or, in other words, that the constructor, whether from parsimony, thoughtlessness, or, as perhaps more frequently happens, from utter ignorance, has neglected either to remove the soil until a solid foundation has been reached, or to strengthen it by the substitution of harder soil or the addition of piling, concrete, or any of the other numerous contrivances so well known to those who have studied the subject. With this explanation of the terms employed it may be laid down as a rule, not universally applicable, but sufficiently so to guide those who have to make inspections or surveys with reference to risk of fire, that after the completion of a building it is impossible or almost impossible to counteract the bad results of natural defects in the soil, and that in general no confidence should be placed in that mysterious, unsatisfactory, and most expensive process known by the vague and unmeaning title "under-pinning," which in point of fact is nothing more or less than a device or trick to hide

Foundation, natural defects of.

Under-pinning.

what is in every case at least a damage, and, as all firemen of experience have frequently and bitterly realised, in many instances an imminent and serious danger. This process, or device, or trick, or whatever it may be called, may possibly be adopted with some degree of safety in small, light, new, and isolated buildings, to obviate defects arising from the ignorance or carelessness of the constructor, but it is wholly inadmissible on a large scale in warehouses or in those long continuous blocks of buildings which form the streets of all great towns. Even when this mode of patching up and concealing a damage is successful, it may be productive of incalculable mischief; as for instance, if a single building of a row or block is under-pinned and the rest allowed to go on in their natural process of sinking, the result almost invariably is a settlement of the walls of the adjoining houses, accompanied by danger in direct proportion to the fracture. Walls may be destroyed by buckling outwards from a thrust or inwards after the falling of the floors, by inherent weakness, absence of proper ties, and in a variety of other ways which will be afterwards explained; but the principal cause of their "tumbling about," to use a fireman's expression, is undoubtedly in almost all cases the want of a proper foundation. The weights carried by different parts of the same wall frequently vary very considerably, and if the ground underneath be all of the same consistency, as is generally the case, some intermediate structure beyond a common foundation is absolutely necessary for buildings liable to be heavily or irregularly loaded. The neglect of this precaution has frequently been the cause of heavy losses.

Under-pinning, danger of.

Walls of adjoining houses, settlement of, through under-pinning.

Walls, buckling, cause of

Unequal weights carried by parts of the same wall.

Intermediate structures, necessity of.

The circumstances under which buildings are erected, and the purposes for which they are intended, vary so much that no general rule can be laid down as to the mode of preparing the foundations, but so far as the results of fires are concerned, great reliance may be placed on walls which are built on inverted arches resting on firm ground, concrete, or any solid sub-structure.

Foundation, solidity of.

Walls built on arches.

A careful inspection of many very heavily and irregularly loaded buildings, even after the shocks, thrusts, and other dangers caused by serious fires, proves most satisfactorily that the kind of foundation here referred to tends in all cases to reduce, and in almost all cases entirely to prevent, fractures and settlements in the walls and consequently communication of smoke and flame.

Fractures and settlements, prevention of.

When a foundation is being prepared, the whole weight of the building and of its probable maximum contents should be calculated, and a very large allowance made for vibration, deterioration from age, shock from falling bodies, &c.

Foundation, weight to be carried by.

Looking to the frightful losses of property, and occasionally of life also, which may be attributed to neglect or ignorance in this way, it would be most desirable that no factory to contain machinery, or warehouse for heavy goods, should be erected to a height exceeding 40 feet, and that no building of any kind should be erected to a height exceeding 50 feet, without a special certificate from a competent architect or surveyor as to the solidity and sufficiency of the foundations.

Building, height of, for carrying heavy goods or machinery.

Buildings, height of, in general.

Indeed it is a subject for very grave consideration whether great benefit would not result from a law to

Architects, desirability of employing.

the effect that no building should be erected within 50 feet of any other building except by a skilled architect, who would be professionally responsible for the strength and sufficiency of all parts of the structure, as well as the foundation.

Whatever opinion, however, may prevail on this subject, there can at least be very little doubt, looking at the matter from a practical point of view, that, as a general rule, a building erected under the advice and supervision of a professional architect ought to be less liable to destruction than one run up without these advantages.

---

4. Area.

This is a subject of considerable importance not only in itself but as one of the elements constituting the cubical capacity. In the first mentioned of these points it is to be judged principally by the distances of the most remote parts from the outside calculated from the entrances or means of approach. Thus, for instance, a building with a superficial area of 10,000 square feet, if constructed on an area of 100 × 100 feet, would have certain points in the inside distant at least 50 feet from any entrance, whereas if it were constructed on an area of 200 × 50, or, to take an extreme case, an area of 1000 × 10 feet, it might be so arranged as to have much greater facility of access. Cubical capacity.

---

5. Height.

The height of a building is a matter of extreme importance also in two ways, which, as in the previous Buildings, height of.

case, will be considered separately; the one with regard to itself alone, the other as forming one of the elements of the cubical capacity.

Buildings, safety of, in proportion to height.

Viewed with regard to itself, it may be laid down that the safety of a building is indirectly as its height; that is to say, that if a building with a capacity of 216,000 cubic feet were erected on an area of 147 × 147 feet to a height of 10 feet, its highest points could be reached without any difficulty, whereas if erected on an area of 46 × 47 feet to a height of 100 feet, its highest point would be exceedingly difficult of access; or to take an extreme case, if erected on a site of 31 × 32 feet to a height of 216 feet, its highest points would be practically quite inaccessible by any of the appliances in ordinary use.

Access to high buildings, difficulty of.

Ladders, external, for high buildings.

Persons who erect high buildings should invariably make their own arrangements for getting down externally to spots within reach of the ladders or other means of escape available from outside.

Ladders, external, wrought iron.

For safety of life it is advisable that all high buildings should be provided with external ladders of wrought iron or some other material likely to be able to resist the effects of a fire at its commencement, and extending to within forty feet of the ground, that being the greatest height at which assistance from without can be promptly rendered.

6. Shape.

Building, shape of.

The safety of a building may be in many instances very considerably influenced by its shape. For instance, a long, narrow building may be altogether burnt out in one part without the other parts being seriously or perhaps at all affected, whereas a square solid building cannot be set on fire in any part without the whole structure becoming seriously endangered. Again, there may be a hollow quadrangular building with good separating walls at the four corners fitted with strong iron or double iron doors which can be closed in case of danger, and yet a fire occurring in one part of such a building may spread to the adjoining wings by passing across the windows of the internal angles.

Fire communicating by angle windows.

To put the subject technically, the several sides of a hollow quadrangular building are naturally within the risk of each other, and, in order to make such a building safe, it is necessary to protect it by strong wrought-iron or other flame-proof and heat-proof shutters capable of covering all the windows near the internal angles.

Shutters, wrought-iron.

It is, therefore, necessary when making a survey to observe specially any points of safety or danger connected with the shape of the building.

7. Cubical Capacity.

In general terms it may be laid down that the risk of a building is in direct proportion to its cubical capacity; that is to say that, all other circumstances being alike, a fire in a building with a capacity of 108,000 cubic feet is much more likely to cause serious damage than in a building of 54,000 cubic feet, and a fire in a building of 216,000 cubic feet is much more likely to cause serious damage than in

Risk of building in proportion to capacity.

one of 108,000 cubic feet; or, to take as before an extreme case, a fire in a building with a capacity of several million cubic feet might, in case of a fire getting to a head, be altogether beyond the reach of any appliances that have yet been made.

Greatest height of building quickly protected.

Greatest cubical capacity quickly protected.

With a well organized and properly equipped fire brigade it is found that sixty feet is the greatest height at which a building can be quickly protected, and that the cube of 60, or 216,000 cubic feet, is the largest cubical capacity which can be protected with reasonable hope of success after a fire has once come to a head.

8. External Walls.

Walls, material for the construction of.

In order to ensure a high degree of safety, walls should be constructed of well-burned bricks, or of some other substance which cannot be affected by fire, as for instance, concrete composed of ashes, slag, or other materials which have been previously burned. Mud forms an excellent fire-proof wall, but unless made to a great thickness it has the disadvantage of getting out of shape when not supported throughout by a frame imbedded within it, and the frame, though necessary for strength, is in itself a source of weakness, as, if made of metal, its expansion and contraction from changes of temperature, though similar in tendency to the expansion and contraction of the mud covering, are different in degree, and consequently lead to fractures sufficient for the admission of smoke and flame.

In the whole range of building materials there is perhaps none so unsuited for resisting fire as that most commonly in use—stone. It is true that, if imbedded in cement or in thoroughly good mortar of lime and sand, it will resist for a considerable time heat gradually applied; but even in such a case it will become calcined, and will crumble to so great an extent as to be unable to carry a load afterwards. In the case of any sudden change of temperature, either from cold to heat or from heat to cold, it cracks instantly without notice, not only leaving a passage for smoke and flame, but in many instances causing the wall to fall. Stone may, however, be used with a certain amount of safety for external walls, but even for this purpose it is very much inferior to bricks.

Stone unsuited for resisting fire

Stone inferior to brick.

Bad mortar is frequently a cause of heavy loss; it has no adhesive power, and consequently fails to bind the other materials in such a way as to prevent buckling. A great quantity of the mortar used in this country during the last fifty years is but little better than road mud, which, though in itself well suited to resist fire, is wanting in the most essential qualities for combining with other materials. Really good mortar becomes in course of time as hard as the bricks or stones, and good cement becomes much harder. In fact, when a hole has to be cut in a wall of bricks laid in sound cement it is generally necessary to cut through the bricks, as the tools in ordinary use for such purposes cannot cut through the cement.

Mortar, quality of.

Cement, strength of.

Walls should be constructed in such a manner as not to separate easily either from defects in the foundation, irregularity of the loads placed on them, vibration, shocks, or other causes. A wall built of

Walls, construction of.

hard bricks laid in sound mortar or cement and properly bonded is perhaps the soundest of all for general purposes, but even such a wall is likely to fail on an emergency, if not firmly bonded into a cross wall.

Enormous losses have been occasioned by the absence of this latter kind of bond; in fact, most

Walls, front and side, parting.

firemen of experience can call to their recollection numerous instances of a front and side wall becoming disconnected at the corner, each falling out separately, and breaking only on contact with the ground, thus showing that, although each may have been a sound

Ties, corner.

wall in itself, the two together were useless as sides of a building for want of a proper corner tie.

It is somewhat curious that, notwithstanding the numerous devices which have been adopted for making walls stand upright, such as buttresses, tie-rods, &c., no instances occur of the attainment of this object by

Walls, zig-zag, construction of.

simply constructing them in a zigzag form with a strong bond at the angles. There are doubtless cases in which such a mode of construction would be in the highest degree inconvenient if not altogether impossible; but, on the other hand, there are many in which the loss of space, loss of material, expense of construction, and inconvenience of approach, would be much less with a thin zigzag wall than with one of those massive costly walls so commonly found, with enormous buttresses blocking up approaches and occupying space.

It is well known that in all boilers or other vessels constructed to resist heavy pressures it is most desirable to avoid having any large flat surfaces, but, notwithstanding this, it is most common to see a whole line of houses with straight front and back walls, although there are cases in which the ties and buttresses alone, which are necessary to obviate the defect of form, are more inconvenient and expensive than the whole wall would be if constructed on the plan here indicated. In a zigzag wall there should be no windows facing each other. In warehouses built on the enormous scale now unfortunately so common, it may frequently be observed that settlements occur sometimes even before the load is put in, and it is therefore worthy of consideration whether the desired result, namely, a wall which can be trusted to stand upright, may not be attained at least occasionally by the substitution of a different construction, in which theoretical correctness of form would not be altogether sacrificed in favour of mere massiveness and bulk.

Buttresses and ties, inconvenience of.

Windows in zigzag walls.

It is a common practice in many large cities to have warehouses of great extent covered over temporarily during their erection, and loaded floor by floor as the buildings proceed, no time being allowed for drying or settling. The requirements of trade are doubtless very urgent, and should not be lightly interfered with or ignored, but the loading of new and unfinished buildings is a most dangerous practice, and liable to lead to very serious results, and it is well known that walls are every day injured beyond any possibility of repair by fracture or settlement resulting from this cause. It may be laid down as a rule, that under no circumstances should a warehouse be loaded with goods, until the mortar has had time to set, and the walls to come to their bearings.

Warehouses, covering during erection.

Warehouses, unfinished, loading.

It is very common at or after fires to see a front and side wall parting from each other, and many instances have occurred in which one or both have fallen down.

This danger can be prevented by having front, back, and side walls properly tied in or bonded to each other. This would have the effect of making all walls which meet at an angle support each other by means of the corner bond alone, without the assistance of floors, joists, roofs, or any of the other ties, which at present appear to constitute their principal strength.

Walls properly tied.

Columns, iron, danger of.

In many places there are corner buildings supported by iron columns only, and therefore most dangerous at any temperature below 31° or above 100° Fahrenheit.

Buildings, corner, supported on iron.

The construction of corner buildings supported on iron alone is dangerous in the extreme, and in order to reduce the danger it is necessary to make it compulsory to place on the outer angle either good walls, brick columns, strong hard wood story posts, or supports of some other material which would be proof against heat.

The same rule applies to internal walls supported on iron columns, as explained in the proper chapter.

Balconies communicating fire.

In rows or streets, verandahs, balconies, or other projections, when constructed of wood or any combustible material, are likely to communicate fire from one house to another, and a continuous row of such projections may bring a whole block of separate buildings into one risk. Notwithstanding this, however, there can be no doubt that continuous balconies, if constructed of wrought iron, or any other material proof against immediate destruction by heat, are most useful for the saving both of life and property. In rows of houses their use is manifest, but even in detached buildings there can be very little doubt that, if sufficiently long, they would serve as a means both of egress for those inside and of access for those giving help from without. It may be assumed that the reason of their not being generally adopted is the double fear which owners of premises have, first, of their servants and other inmates getting out too frequently; and, secondly, of persons breaking in for improper purposes; but those who guard themselves so carefully from these dangers should remember at what cost they do so, and should be prepared to accept the results of a fire causing loss of life or property as the direct and inevitable consequence of their own state of preparation.

The area of all the apertures in a wall, such as doors, windows, &c., should on no account exceed the total area of solid wall in which they are placed. Apertures, area of.

Bond timber in walls is dangerous and should not be allowed. When it rots or burns, there is a tendency in the walls to crack. Bond timbers in walls, danger of.

Hoop iron forms a much better bond, and is free from the drawbacks attending the use of wood. Bonds, hoop-iron.

Lean-to buildings are dangerous if there are windows in the wall above them. Buildings, lean-to.

Weather boarding causes two dangers, one of taking fire from without, the other of conveying fire through the windows. Weather boarding.

Wherever iron is used it must be allowed sufficient play for its elasticity and also for the expansion and contraction which it undergoes unceasingly in consequence of changes of temperature. Iron, elasticity of.

In some countries it is the custom to encase the Bressummers.

ends of a bressummer in cast-iron shoes, but this is a very bad practice, and should not be permitted, as the iron would convey fire rapidly from one side to the other.

Walls, external and return, to be properly tied.

An external wall should be firmly tied to party and return walls by strong wrought-iron anchors, of sufficient strength and number to keep the whole outside of the building firmly fixed without the assistance of floors, roofs, or internal ties of any kind.

Brick and stone, combination of.

It is by no means improbable that some of the destruction or damage in walls after fires has been in many cases owing to the vicious practice, latterly so common, of endeavouring to make buildings seem different from what they really are.

Thus, for instance, the walls of a most imposing and pretentious building of sufficient thickness, and apparently constructed of sound stone, are found to crack at an early stage of a fire, and perhaps to fall down altogether eventually, and then it is discovered that they have been only a deception, having been constructed externally of stone and internally of brick.

In such cases also it is generally to be observed, that if the walls had been composed of stone alone, or of brick alone, they would almost certainly have stood, whereas with the two materials combined they not only failed, but began to do so at a very early stage, thus seeming to indicate that uniformity of strength in walls cannot be obtained without uniformity of construction, and to a very large extent a precise uniformity in the power of the materials used to resist pressure, or, in other words, to carry weight; for it is obvious that if the inner part of a wall which

Construction uniformity of.

carries the floors and their contents becomes compressed, however slightly, while the outer part is not so affected, there must be a separation of the two, and as a consequence imminent danger to the building and its contents, and also to those engaged in extinguishing the fire.

The anchors to be used at each end of every plate piece should be worked into the side, end, or party walls of a building, and the ends of the anchors should turn up and down at least several inches. Anchors to be worked in.

It must always be a very serious question how far processes or operations carried on within a building have a chemical effect on the materials of which the walls are constructed. It seems certain that strong volatile vapours, such as those evolved from alcohol and other spirits, spirit oils, and many liquids of various kinds in common use, have some effect on mortar and cement, and this should be a subject for careful scientific observation in large buildings used for distillation and other purposes, involving the continuance of a high temperature for many years and a more or less free discharge of pungent chemical vapours. Material, chemical effect on. Distillation, buildings used for.

In most regulations thickness of walls for various circumstances is defined, but it is obvious that this cannot always be correct, as the pressure must vary very considerably according as the surface of the ground is level or inclined, and also in many other ways. Walls, thickness o

Wherever iron is used either for bressumers or in walls, as for beams, joists, &c., proper allowance must be made for its expansion and contraction with changes of temperature. If this is not attended to, Elasticity of iron, allowance to be made for.

serious fractures may be caused in the walls, and sometimes destruction.

Walls of loaded buildings, anchors for.

Anchors fastening the corner walls of loaded buildings should generally not be more than about ten feet apart.

Walls of buildings to carry machinery, anchors for.

Where walls of buildings intended to carry a heavy load or to withstand the vibration of machinery are built in isolated or nearly isolated piers, there should be strong inverted arches turned under and between the piers.

Balconies uninflammable.

In continuous buildings of great height rows of balconies of some uninflammable material on all the floors are the most effectual means for saving life.

Mortar.

There are many kinds of good cement for resisting fire, and, where none of these can be obtained, mortar compounded of sharp clean sand or grit, and good lime in proper proportions, will be found very effectual in resisting the effects of heat and flame.

Walls tied together by floors and roof.

Walls should under no circumstances be tied together by the floors or roofs; but, where there are return walls, these should be firmly tied or bonded with the external walls. Many very serious losses may be attributed to the insufficiency of this kind of bond.

Chimney breasts, foundation of

Chimney breasts ought to be laid on a firm foundation at the base, and tied at every story to the wall supporting them. Where this cannot be done, and where it is necessary to corbel out a portion of a wall to carry them, the wall should be strengthened at its foundation immediately below the corbel, and also throughout its whole height to the top. As this latter mode is almost impossible in an old building, the natural inference is that in general it is most undesirable to add chimneys to old buildings. Chimneys added to old buildings.

The height to which party or fire walls should be carried above a roof depends very much on the height and size of the building. Thus, for instance, 15 inches are sometimes found enough in moderate-sized dwellings, whereas 10 feet have been found insufficient in large, high, and heavily loaded warehouses. Walls, party, height of, above roof.

In cases where bressummers rest on party walls, they should be borne on templates or corbels of brick or iron, tailed through at least half the thickness of the walls and of the full breadth of the bressummers. The use of stone as a corbel for this purpose is quite inadmissible, but where there is a solid stone wall the bressummer may be laid across the whole breadth of the wall, and, so far as only the carrying of the load is concerned, will be found to stand very well in this way. Bressummers borne on corbels of brick.

This latter mode, however, is applicable only to isolated buildings, and ought never to be adopted in rows or streets, as it involves the risk of communicating fire to adjoining premises by means of the bressummers. In rows of buildings no part of any bressummer should be placed nearer than within 4½ inches of the centre of the party wall, thus allowing the space of 9 inches, or that of a full-sized brick, between the bressummers of adjoining houses. Bressummers communicating fire.

Copings, balconies, cornices, or other projections should never be constructed of stone, as this material is certain to fall down at an early stage of a fire, and is likely to kill both persons endeavouring to escape and those coming to render aid. Projections, construction of.

Wherever such projections are placed, and whatever

material they may be composed of, they should invariably be well supported from the inside, and should be of a weight in proper proportion to the strength and tenacity of the internal supports.

Projections securing.

Cornices and other projections of the same kind are very dangerous when the internal supports are burned away, and the bond stones by which they are generally fastened to the walls are of no use when flames are coming out of the windows underneath.

This is a point very much neglected in many large buildings, but it is one of paramount importance in connection with fires.

Walls, hollow.

Hollow walls should contain as much brick, stone, or other material as if they were solid, but even with this precaution they can seldom be made safe for carrying loads or withstanding the effects of vibration.

Walls anchored to beams.

The practice adopted in some countries of anchoring walls to each tier of beams is one of most doubtful utility. Properly walls should be anchored to each other and to nothing else, and in such a case floors might be burned or fall without affecting them.

Mortar, action of frost on.

Walls should not be built during frost, as the mortar when freezing will not adhere to the bricks or stones, and in case of fire the walls will tumble down altogether from want of adhesion of the parts.

Cornices, danger of.

Cornices or other projections if made of wood or other combustible materials are always dangerous even for a single house, but for a row they are much more dangerous, as they are very likely to communicate fire rapidly from one house to the next. Where they exist in a continuous row, they should be carefully cut and separated by several feet of some incombustible material, but even with this precaution they must always be considered dangerous.

Cornices are always dangerous in case of fire, but the danger is much diminished if they are built with an equal weight of material inside and outside the centre of the wall, so that their tendency should be to balance and not to fall in either direction. If the weights are unequal the greater weight should be on the inside in order to prevent loss of life.

All cornices should be firmly hung on or otherwise secured by iron anchors. These anchors should be several feet long, including an angle of the proper length, and should be worked or built into the side or end walls of the building; the anchors used for supporting the centre of a cornice should return down the front of the building on the inner side, and be firmly secured in the wall itself, and not, as is commonly the case, merely to the front beam. Cornices, securing. Cornices, anchors for securing.

9. Roofs.

In numerous cases the roofs of buildings in this country consist of a wooden frame covered over with tiles or slates; and in many large warehouses the frames, which are of massive timber, are first planked over, and the planking then covered with slates or lead, or both. Roofs, covering for.

Again, in some buildings there is left between the roof and the ceiling of the top room a large space, to which access is difficult, and which may consequently conceal the elements of danger until they become serious. It is difficult to understand the principle on Roofs, space between ceiling and.

which those persons act, who, after constructing and covering in for themselves a building of a certain size, deliberately deprive themselves of the use of a large portion of it; but as long as peaked roofs are constructed over flat ceilings this must, of course, be the case, and danger must ensue; but even when these spaces are utilised, as they sometimes are, for storage of old furniture, &c. &c., the danger is greatly aggravated.

Roofs, access to the inside of.

All firemen of experience can recall to their recollection numerous instances of either total losses of buildings or very serious damage, caused entirely by the absence of any means of access to the inside of roofs.

Access to roof, danger arising from having no.

It is not very long since a most valuable old public building was almost entirely destroyed in this way. The firemen, with a large force of engines and an abundant supply of water, were at work for a considerable time endeavouring to obtain access to the inside of the roof and finally the roof and ceiling both fell into the body of the building, almost entirely destroying the furniture, fittings, and a considerable portion of the valuable property. In this case the loss was altogether owing to the unnecessary strength of the roof, and the great inflammability of the materials of which it was composed.

Roofs, lengths of, without divisions.

One of the greatest dangers at present in this country is the enormous lengths of roof constructed of massive timber in a very dry condition and without divisions, but this can be to a considerable extent obviated by completing existing walls and chimney stacks so as to convert them into fire walls. In doing this the greatest care must be taken, not only to remove from them as far as possible all bond timber and wood

Walls, existing, converting.

plates, but also to cut a piece of at least three or four inches out of every bressummer, beam, joist, purlin, or other timber, where it passes through a wall, so that fire could not communicate from one side to the other.

It is possible that there may be an objection in certain spots to bringing walls through roofs, and in such cases the walls may be brought at least up to the roof, and all the timber cut and separated as before mentioned, and the slates laid on good solid mortar on the top of the wall so as to prevent communication of fire.

This mode, though much inferior to the other, will be a very considerable improvement on the ordinary construction of roofs as far as regards risk of fire.

The roofs, now so common, constructed of massive timber, planked over and covered with slates, might, in buildings exceeding a certain size, be done away with, and roofs of corrugated iron or other light metal (Roofs, iron, corrugated.) substituted for them, with sliding or other windows, which, when necessary, could be opened to let the smoke and heat rise, and so enable the firemen to get at their work inside, without which they never can succeed in extinguishing a fire without heavy loss. The roofs might be laid on light iron trusses, some- (Roofs, iron, construction of.) what in the form of the lattice girders now so exten-tensively used in railway bridges, and each of these might be plated over like the bulkhead of an iron ship, and pass through the roof, thus forming a complete party or fire wall as far as it goes, and subdividing the roof into compartments, which might be fitted with (Roofs, iron, subdividing.) iron doors to enable the firemen and others to pass through in case of need.

Roofs of iron, effect of building. The effect of this arrangement would be to make iron to a certain extent change its place in future buildings, being used exclusively in the roof, where it has to carry only its own weight, and being partially removed from the floors, where the load is heavy, and its place supplied and strength supplemented by occasional wooden story posts or brick columns, which would insure the floors standing much longer than they do at present in case of fire.

Roofs, openings in. For safety of life all roofs should be provided with dormer windows or other openings, and proper means of access to them should always be available.

Roofs, trapdoors in. Where there are trapdoors leading into and through roofs, it is very much the custom to have them at the top of the stairs; but there are serious evils attending them in this position, as the whole draught of a fire commonly sets upwards through the well of a staircase, and drives smoke, heat, and flame to the top with great fury and rapidity. It is occasionally found that flames break their way through a roof at that part over the well of a staircase before even the light panelling of the doors on the landings below have been burned through, and thus it is plain that this spot, although very useful for discharging smoke and heat, is by no means the most suitable for a place of exit for the occupiers of a building. A much safer mode for the escape of persons is to have the trapdoor leading out of each of the top rooms, or out of one to which all the others have access, so that persons coming from the lower floors could retreat into any of these rooms, and by shutting the door after them exclude the smoke and heat, and thus very considerably increase their time for escape.

Roofs, position of trapdoors in.

Escape by means of trapdoors.

Projecting woodwork of a roof is likely to take fire from windows below. Projecting woodwork of roof.

In rows of houses with ridge and furrow roofs the party walls should rise from the top of the ridge, not from the bottom of the furrow. Many valuable buildings have been lost in consequence of neglect on this point.

In a continuous line of large buildings with ridge and valley roofs it is particularly advisable to have the party walls placed at the ridges and not in the valleys, as, if raised high enough from the valleys to separate the risks of two adjoining ridges, they may be too high for the firemen to reach over without ladders, or for persons who have reached their own roof to escape over to the next.

---

10. Internal Divisions.

The internal divisions are to a house what the party walls are to a block or street. It seems to be acknowledged by all who have studied the question that party walls should be complete, but it never seems to have been thoroughly understood that although internal divisions cannot be made complete without great inconvenience, they may nevertheless be made to a certain extent, in many cases to a very great extent, sufficiently complete to help to stop fires spreading. It is, of course, out of the question to expect ordinary houses to be cut up into a number of perfect divisions; but, where there are walls, there seems to be no reason why they should not be made as complete as possible,

Divisions, internal.

Divisions, internal, incomplete.

without interfering with the purposes for which the building is used.

Divisions, internal, complete.

The more divisions there are in a building, the safer the building is. If the divisions are vertical, quite complete, and numerous, there may be a very great amount of safety; if they are horizonal, incomplete, and less numerous, there would be less safety; but in either case the safety is in exact proportion to the position, completeness, and number of the divisions.

Divisions, internal, material for.

The material of which the partitions are constructed is, of course, a matter of great importance, substances which are not combustible or likely to be influenced by the effects of heat being much better suited than those which can be burned, calcined, or otherwise injured by fire; but, whatever may be the material employed, it is certain that the safety of a building is always in direct proportion to the number and completeness of its internal divisions.

Buildings, large, in one risk.

Internal divisions are often made without the smallest regard to the spread of fire, and all the parts of many enormous buildings are thus frequently found to be in one risk; that is to say, not to contain any party wall or other complete separation which would of itself cut off a fire; and this is the more remarkable when in many cases their own style and dimensions plainly show that great facilities must have originally existed for at least a partial protection in this way.

Buildings, subdivision of, after completed.

One of the principal difficulties in dealing with the subject in question is the obvious fact that a proper and complete subdivision of many buildings after their construction into a number of small risks would be impossible without a vast expenditure of money, and in many cases the utter ruin of some of perhaps the most beautiful and important features of the architecture, including, perhaps, corridors, galleries, and, in some instances, suites of rooms. While, therefore, the necessity is recognised of avoiding generally any measures which would totally alter the character and style of architecture, there, nevertheless, remains the fact that much may frequently be done to reduce the danger of a fire spreading by a partial separation wherever it is found possible, particularly in the roof and upper portions of buildings. Separations, partial.

With this view spots may often be selected for partitions which will be found to correspond almost exactly with existing walls or chimney stacks, and in each of these spots, or as many of them as practicable, a party wall as complete as possible may be constructed passing up to and, wherever allowable, through the roof to a convenient height on the outside. Partitions, spots to be selected for building.

In upper stories and roofs there is generally no difficulty and comparatively little expense in carrying out this plan so as to effectually divide that part of the structure into a number of different risks, no one of which would be unmanageable in case of fire, and then the only incomplete portion of the party or fire walls would be in the lower floors, where, owing to the construction and contents of the buildings, there may be much less risk; but it is probable that even in these parts there may be found a few spots where, without seriously interfering with the character of the architecture, iron doors or revolving iron shutters may be placed, or at least double oak doors with an interval between, which, on an emergency, might be filled with wet bedding or blankets so as to check the spread of fire, and at every such spot the flooring should be cut Roofs, subdividing. Doors, iron. Shutters, iron, revolving. Doors, oak, double.

Flooring separated by plaster.

and separated by plaster, or some other uninflammable material.

Brick or iron, use of.

The floors, jambs, and heads of doorways may in most cases be safely formed of brick or iron, but should on no account be of stone, as this latter material has no power of resisting the effects of fire.

Divisions, internal, openings in.

Openings of internal divisions should be fitted with single or double wrought-iron doors, which should be of sufficient thickness according to their area, and should be strengthened by ribs, rails, or bars, also of wrought iron. These doors should be closely fitted to strong wrought-iron frames in the apertures, and should be mounted with bolts, hinges, locks, or other supports of the number, size, and strength necessary to keep them in their places when exposed to heat.

Doors, iron, supports for.

The supports should be of best wrought iron or steel, and should not be more distant from each other than two feet measured along the edge of the doors.

Doors, iron, danger of insufficient supports for.

Some of the most disastrous fires which have ever taken place owe their extent to the warping or buckling of iron doors for want of proper support in the frames.

Shutters, iron, revolving.

When it is inconvenient or impossible to fix iron doors, it is often very useful to mount over the openings revolving iron shutters which are comparatively light, weighing only about 14 lbs. to the superficial square foot. They can be made moderately air-tight, and, to a certain extent, impervious to fire, and can be raised and lowered with the greatest ease by means of a worm and wheel, or by a simple arrangement of pulleys and counterweights.

No internal division wall of brick can be relied on

to resist shocks unless its thickness is at least two thirds of that of the external walls, and to resist fire in large, heavily-loaded buildings it should, under no circumstances, be less than 9 inches. Divisions, internal, thickness of.

No internal wall built on iron columns or supported by iron can be relied on where there is much heat. Columns, iron, walls, built on.

Stone is permissible for the sill or floor under an iron door, but it is a most unsafe material for the doorhead or lintel. In the former case it acts as a medium for separating the floors of rooms, and it carries nothing; therefore, when it becomes cracked or calcined, which it is certain to do when subjected to heat, no bad consequences happen; whereas, in the latter case, it breaks and falls down, bringing with it, perhaps, the whole or a portion of the wall, and allowing fire to pass through freely. Stone, cases in which it may be used.

The internal divisions of a house, if made of light or combustible materials, should be covered with a coating of plaster sufficiently thick to prevent or delay the action of fire. Combustible material of buildings to be covered by plaster.

Counting-houses, offices, sample-rooms, and sale-rooms in warehouses, being kept open later than those parts of the buildings used for the storage or deposit of goods, should be separated from such parts either by solid walls of brick or stone, or by double iron doors. Offices, separation of.

In theatres and other places for the reception and entertainment of large numbers of persons, involving the carrying on of manufacturing processes, such as carpentering, glueing, &c., &c., the storage of dangerous stocks of highly inflammable materials, and the use of large quantities of light, there is much room for improvement. Theatres, manufacturing processes in.

A simple arrangement might be made to divide

Theatres, divisions in, by means of party wall and revolving iron shutters.

such places into at least two distinct risks, the stage workshops and stores being in one and the audience in the other.

This could be accomplished by building a complete party or fire wall across the whole building except where the curtain hangs, and close by the curtain might be suspended a revolving iron shutter with a considerable overlap, which could be lowered at a moment's notice to cut off the risk from one portion of the building, thus insuring to the firemen and others an immediate entry to at least a portion of the premises, and so enabling them to give early and effective aid.

Prohibition to work or store in roofs.

The roofs, which are now the most dangerous parts of such places, might with advantage be constructed of iron or other light metal, and divided as before mentioned, and it should be absolutely prohibited to use any portion of the roof, as at present, for either workshops or storerooms.

Inflammability.

The curtains, wings, flies, slides, the whole of the stage, and many other parts, might be occasionally washed or soaked in a mixture of alum and water, or some similar substance, which would have the effect of rendering them less inflammable, and, even in the event of their catching fire, would entirely prevent that sudden blazing up which at present constitutes the great risk in all such places.

Theatres, walls in, to be perforated and fitted with iron doors.

The transverse fire wall should be perforated at every floor, even to the basement under the stage, and the openings fitted with double wrought-iron doors. Every door for exit should be made to open outwards, and such a space allowed for this purpose that the building could be cleared of the whole audience within five minutes of the time of giving an alarm.

Theatres, exit of audience from.

If, in addition to this, a separate place of exit were provided for each floor or landing, the probability of a serious panic, with the delay consequent thereon, would be much reduced, the firemen would be enabled to get to their work sooner, and would, no doubt, be more successful in stopping a serious fire than they can hope to be under the existing arrangements.

No building can be considered to be properly divided, which is fitted with lifts or moveable rooms in the middle of the floors, or with trapdoors in the floors. Lifts and trapdoors in floors.

Wherever iron doors are used, some person should be held responsible for having them properly closed and secured at night, and at all times when the premises are left by the caretakers. Serious losses have resulted from neglect of this precaution. Doors, iron, closing.

11. Chimneys.

For those parts of a chimney which are supported throughout, stone may under some circumstances be admissible, but brick is always preferable for the purpose. Chimneys, brick preferable for.

The abutments of a chimney should be tied in to the walls by wrought-iron bars of sufficient number and strength, turned up and down at the ends, and built into the jambs for several inches on each side. Chimneys, abutments of.

No part of a flue should be of less thickness than half a brick or 4½ inches. Flues, thickness of.

Where slabs of stone or slate are placed level with a floor before the opening of a chimney, they should invariably be laid in sound mortar, cement, or other Hearth-stone, setting.

incombustible and non-conducting substance, and should be at a distance of not less than 4½ inches from the joists, flooring, or any other wood work.

Chimneys built up to the roof.

A chimney built only up to the roof and stopping at that point is always dangerous.

Imperfect draft.

A flue with such imperfect draft that the smoke occasionally or frequently blows downwards is never safe, as the kindling or fuel is likely to be blown out of the grate and set fire to the room.

Chimneys, removing bricks from.

The practice of removing bricks from a chimney in order to prevent it smoking is highly dangerous and should be prohibited.

Flues, blocked-up.

It is always dangerous to block up a fireplace or flue; the proper course is to build it up altogether, and thus prevent sparks falling or soot or dust accumulating.

Chimneys, separate.

Every chimney in a house should be perfectly distinct and separate from every other chimney from the hearth to the external opening. Chimneys may safely be built in stacks, but they should on no account have any connexion within the stacks.

Flues, thickness of brickwork round.

Brickwork around flues should not be less than 4½ inches thick in any part.

By the Code Napoléon it was not permitted to build a chimney against the wall of an adjoining house without isolating it by an intermediate wall of sufficient thickness to prevent heat passing to the neighbouring premises.

12. Staircases and Stairs.

Staircases and stairs, construction of.
Staircase, rooms opening on.
Rooms built in suites.
Fire, escape from.

The position and construction of staircases and stairs are matters of great importance. If, as most commonly happens in this country, every room opens on to some part of the staircase, it is obvious that a very small quantity of materials on fire in the hall or lower part of the house may have the effect of cutting off all possibility of escape by the stairs; whereas, if rooms are built in suites of three or four together with only one door opening on the staircase, persons endangered may retreat from one to another, defending themselves as they go by piling up bedding, wet blankets, or other materials calculated to arrest the progress of the flames and smoke, and thus obtaining additional time for help to reach them from without. In all countries where this mode of construction is adopted there is a corresponding immunity from heavy loss of life.

Stairs, material for building.

The material also of which stairs are constructed should be a subject for serious consideration. Any materials imbedded on a solid substructure would be comparatively safe, although the substructure itself might be of a combustible nature, but as apart from the expense there is very rarely space for such a construction, it is necessary to consider the subject from the point of view exhibited in ordinary buildings.

Stairs, safety of.

Stairs laid on solid walls of brick, stone, earth, or concrete, are almost absolutely safe under all circumstances which may be expected to arise, whethert he steps are composed of bricks, stones, slabs of slate, wood, wrought iron, cast iron, or any of the other materials in common use. It is only when these materials are not supported, or, to put the case in other words, when they have to support themselves, that the enormous difference in their power of resisting the effects of heat becomes manifest.

Stairs, self-supporting.

Viewed in this light, they may be placed in the following order, bricks being put out of the question, as from their very nature they cannot be used except for a solid structure.

Stairs, material for building.

Wrought iron is the best material of all; cast iron the next best, then come the various kinds of wood, particularly the hard woods, such as oak, elm, ash, mahogany, &c.; after these come slabs of slate, which will be found to stand considerable heat; and last of all stone, which for such a purpose is utterly and entirely inadmissible. It may be necessary to mention that this strong opinion is not given in ignorance of the fact that for many years past the kinds of construction here condemned has not only received legislative sanction, but has in certain cases been made absolutely compulsory. It is, perhaps, now useless to inquire by what authority, under what circumstances, or for what supposed useful purpose, such expressions have been introduced into acts of Parliament as "stone or other fireproof materials," or how such provisions have been introduced as those which make it compulsory to construct "floors of lobbies, corridors, passages, and landings, and also flights of stairs," of this most dangerous of all materials whether considered as to its property of intrinsic strength, strength for withstanding shocks, power of resisting heat, or in fact any other qualification except appearance; but it is by

Staircases, stone inadmissible for.

no means useless to continue to combat the principles on which these terms have been introduced, or to endeavour to lay down others which may lead to a diminution of the constant and serious dangers resulting from them. It is not too much to say that any enactment which contains such an expression as "stone or other fireproof material" proceeds on an asumption involving a serious error, inasmuch as stone is in no possible sense fireproof, but on the contrary yields to the effects of fire more rapidly than almost any other material commonly used for building. It is true that it does not, like wood, add fuel to the fire, but it does worse, as its known tendency to split off from the walls, and fall down altogether, prevents the firemen from availing themselves of the best positions for their work, which they can almost always occupy where there are wooden staircases. For a staircase on the outside of a building stone may possibly be used with some kind of safety, but its brittleness, when exposed to different degrees of heat in different parts, makes it an unsafe material for inside staircases or lobbies, which are liable in case of fire to undergo a sudden expansion in the tread or exposed part, while the support or part resting inside the wall is scarcely raised in temperature; or, if they escape this danger and get hot so slowly as not to break, the draft of cold air caused by opening a door or window is quite sufficient to contract and split the stone. In both cases the fracture occurs in the same place, close to the wall.

Stone not fireproof.

Stone, tendency of, to split.

No staircase can be considered really fireproof unless constructed either of fire-bricks laid in fire-cement, which would be both costly and cumbrous, or of wrought iron, which for appearance, comfort, or

Staircases, wrought-iron.

convenience, might be covered with slabs of slate, stone, or wood. In this latter case the real strength would consist, not in the stone or other covering, but in the wrought-iron framing, and such a stairs, particularly if protected by plaster, which could be easily done, might safely be relied on in all ordinary fires, as the heat near a staircase, being tempered with the cold draft from the outside, is rarely sufficient to weaken wrought iron, which only fuses at a temperature of about 3000° Fahrenheit, and retains a considerable portion of its strength almost to the melting point. The fact of the law asserting that stone is a fireproof material suited for lobbies, stairs, &c., has done incalcuble injury, as may be observed at the scene of any fire in a building so constructed, particularly if there have been both wooden and stone stairs, in which case it almost invariably happens that some portion of the wooden stairs is saved, while the stone is completely destroyed, and generally discovered afterwards among the ruins in the basement.

Iron, wrought, strength of.

Staircases, superiority of wood over stone.

It is, therefore, necessary to impress on all concerned that this mode of construction is based on a grave error, and is certain always to do, as it already has done, most serious injury to life and property. The only way in which an unsupported stone staircase can be saved in a building on fire is to flood it with water at an early stage, and this must always occupy the careful attention of the firemen at a time when their efforts would otherwise be exerted in a totally different direction.

Staircases, stone, subjected to heat.

No fireman of large experience has ever seen a stone staircase escape when subjected to much heat, and, this being the case, it would seem to be most desirable that there should be introduced a prohibition of the use of stone as a material for lobbies, corridors, passages, landings, or stairs, except where it is supported throughout and not overhanging in any part.

It is again repeated that the use of stone is most dangerous for this purpose, except when it is supported throughout.

Steps, stone, dangerous.

Ordinary stone steps are most dangerous, as their strength entirely depends on their being kept at the common temperature of the atmosphere; in other words, they are dependent on the power of the iron doors to resist the fire; and, when these fail or are left open, and the flames burst through, the whole of the stairs above that level are crumbled into fragments in a moment, and would of course kill every one whose duty it might be to be at work on or under them at the time.

Stairs, stone, built solid.

It may be laid down as a rule that of all building materials stone is the least able to resist the effects of fire. It may be safely used for walls, because in that case it is supported throughout, or it may be used for stairs, provided that they are built solid, but for stairs in the ordinary sense of the word, that is to say, steps with one end pinned into a wall, and the other end hanging and unsupported, stone is a most dangerous material to use. In short, under no circumstances at all can it be considered fireproof, whether used for stairs or any other purpose.

Stairs, wooden, destruction of.

Wooden stairs are generally destroyed only when they contain within them a sort of funnel or chamber which carries the fire from one part to another, and when they are set in the walls or other supports, with their ends covered by skirting boards with a passage for air inside.

Stairs, wooden, plaster underneath.

A wooden stairs well plastered underneath, and without hidden air funnels, will stand a very considerable amount of fire.

While these lines were being written, a notable instance occurred of the almost complete destruction of a large and valuable building in consequence of the stairs yielding to a heat, which would not have had a perceptible effect on almost any other building material, and certainly would not have caused serious inconvenience to any experienced fireman. Just as the men were about to mount, the iron banisters and the steps began to come down, first singly and in fragments, afterwards in positive showers resembling the firing of shot and shell from heavy guns, many of the parts descending from the highest levels with such force as to become imbedded in the plaster and panelling of the lower walls. Fortunately there were means of immediate escape for the men, but only for themselves, as they were obliged to abandon their appliances, which instantly became imbedded in the heap. An entrance with fresh appliances was soon effected into the higher floors by means of ladders from the outside, but by that time the place had been nearly burned out.

Stairs, stone, destruction of.

---

13. Floors.

Floors, special construction of.

Floors should be specially constructed for what they have to carry. Thus, for instance, a floor for a warehouse containing heavy goods should be much stronger than a floor which has to carry only light goods; and again a floor of any warehouse should be stronger than that of an ordinary private house of moderate dimensions.

This statement may seem superfluous and unnecessary to any one considering the subject from an abstract point of view, as it is obvious, that the only alternative would be to build every floor of sufficient strength to carry the heaviest goods, or the weight of the largest number of persons that could be closely packed together, or both combined, and in addition able to withstand exceptional shocks and thrusts from machinery, movement of persons, goods, &c., and that on account of the expense alone, independently of other contingencies, this alternative would be wholly out of the question.

It is, however, by no means superfluous to those, who are forced to consider the subject in connexion with the existing condition of buildings, and who are professionally engaged in obviating the consequences of careless and defective construction, and of those changes in the uses of buildings which are unfortunately permitted in many great cities.

Floors supported on stone projections.

The next points, after the intrinsic strength of the floors, are the nature, style, and strength of their supports. A floor supported, as is frequently the case, on nothing but stone projections can never be trusted after the temperature has been suddenly raised to any considerable extent.

Floors, sleepers for.

When the surrounding walls are of stone, a continuous stone projection all round is permissible, as the chances are against the whole splitting and falling together, but even in this case it is much safer to have a longitudinal piece of wrought iron or hard wood laid as a sleeper above the stone.

Floors, safest support for.

The safest description of lateral support for floors is to have a portion of the walls corbelled out in brick, which will never yield to heat, whether applied gradually or suddenly.

Floors, intermediate supports for.

Floors which have a very large area or have to carry heavy loads should invariably be provided with central or intermediate supports, and the more these are made of some material which can resist the effects of heat the better. For this purpose wood of any kind, but especially hard wood, is infinitely preferable to stone or iron.

Intermediate supports, material for.

Floors, cast-iron, columns for supporting.

Cast-iron columns, in consequence of the small space they occupy, are now much used for supporting floors of warehouses and shops, where light and room are of great consequence, and their strength is usually calculated according to the weight which they are designed to carry, the breaking strain being generally considerably over the load, thus allowing a sufficient margin for exceptional contingencies such as vibration, or the falling of heavy bales of goods; but in this calculation the question of any other temperature than that of the ordinary atmosphere appears to have been lost sight of altogether, and when it is remembered that, at a temperature of 212° Fahrenheit, or the boiling point of water, cast iron loses about 15 per cent. of its strength; that, at the temperature of molten lead 612° Fahrenheit, it has probably no strength at all; and that, at a temperature of 2787° Fahrenheit, which is probably much below that of the centre of a large building on fire, it becomes liquid, it seems advisable to supplement this material with some other more trustworthy in case of heat.

Temperature at which iron loses its strength.

When it is necessary to use iron columns, they will

be found much more capable of resisting the effects of heat if made solid and not hollow, as is most commonly the case.

Columns, if used, to be solid.

For the purpose of support an occasional brick column would answer best, but, as there would certainly be much objection to the space it would occupy and the consequent obstruction of light, it appears hopeless in ordinary cases to expect it to be done; however, in floors exceeding a certain size, say 100 by 50 feet, there would probably be no such objection, and in all others one wooden story post might with advantage be substituted for every fourth iron column. For the story post oak or elm would be the best timber to use, and the remaining iron columns might be to a considerable extent protected by plaster.

Supports, intermediate.

Iron columns protected by plaster.

It is somewhat unfortunate that of late years the words fireproof and incombustible have been used indifferently, and it must be acknowledged that some existing acts of Parliament have given legislative sanction to the error.

These are, however, by no means synonymous terms; on the contrary, there are many cases in which combustible substances are much more proof against fire than non-combustible, as an instance of which may be cited the acknowledged fact, proved by long experience in this and other countries, and now placed beyond doubt, that good oak or other hard wood posts with girders and joists filled well in with proper concrete prepared for the purpose come nearer to practical fireproofing than any arrangement of iron combined with brick or stone hitherto brought into use.

Terms combustible and fireproof.

Floors should invariably be brought in so close to the walls that there should be no possibility of either

Floors brought close in to the walls.

flame or smoke passing, even when the joists or other supports spring and buckle as they frequently do during fires from the weight of either water resting on them, large bodies of men moving about, or heavy weights falling on them. Skirting boards are quite unnecessary for any properly constructed floors except for the purposes of ornament, to which these remarks have of course no reference.

Floors, material for.

The material of which floors are most commonly constructed is wood, but they may in certain cases be safely made of slate, or still more safely of brick or various kinds of concrete on supports which can resist the effects of heat. Stone is a very bad material for flooring except when bedded ou a foundation of solid earth or some other fireproof and non-conducting substance.

Air, circulatiou of.

Circulatiou of air should on no account be permitted in any part of a building not exposed to view, especially under floors, or inside skirting boards or wainscots.

Floors, plaster for protecting.

Good plaster protects wood and other inflammable materials from fire almost perfectly, and a sound pugging of plaster between the ceiling of a room and the floor of that over is practically found impervious to flame.

Floors, air and water-tight.

The floors of a building of whatever material they are constructed should be made both air-tight and water-tight, and they would in this way resist the effects of heat much longer than if this precaution is omitted. They might with advantage even be caulked like a ship's deck, only with dry oakum without pitch.

Floors, caulked.

14. Number and Size of Separate Risks.

An important element in calculating the safety or danger of a building is the internal arrangement, which may be made with partitions so constructed as to divide the whole into several distinct and separate parts, each quite safe from any possible effect of fires in the others, or to partially divide the separate portions so that although a fire might if left to itself go through from one to another, nevertheless there would be points at which it could be cut off by firemen, or which might be simply without any partitions at all, in which case the whole building is said to be in one risk. Risks, division of.

As a general rule the more partitions there are the better, and the more complete the divisions are the better. Even the lightest wood, although when ignited it adds fuel to the fire, is often very effectual in checking and sometimes in stopping a draft, and thus saving great destruction of property. Partitions, number of.

In many large warehouses and manufactories the work could not be carried on if there were partitions, and, therefore, such places are built entirely in one risk, and, of course, the proprietors have to take the consequences, either in the shape of a high premium if they are insured, or of a probability of serious loss in the event of a fire happening if uninsured. Fire, probability of loss by.

There are, however, many buildings at present in one risk which might be completely divided into several, and many others which might be partially so divided, Risk, division of.

without in any way interfering with the purposes for which they are constructed.

Separations, incomplete. There are again others which present the singular and unaccountable anomaly of having perfectly sound, strong, and well-constructed external walls and a considerable number of internal divisions, but these latter made without the smallest regard to the spread of fire, and consequently the whole being practically in one risk, that is to say, not containing any party wall or other complete separation which would of itself cut off a fire.

---

15. Nature of Stock.

Stock, nature of. The risk of fire in a building depends much more on the nature of the stock than is commonly supposed, so much so, indeed, that the term fireproof, so frequently used, is absolutely without meaning as applied to the structure alone, unless the structure may happen to be empty.

This point must therefore be carefully examined before estimating a risk, and it must be kept quite separate from another and a more important one to be considered hereafter under the head of business carried on, inasmuch as this latter generally involves the double risk of stock and manufacture combined.

Goods, stowage of. In many cases buildings are stocked with goods in such a way that only persons whose business it is to be constantly in them can find their way about even in broad daylight and under circumstances in every way favorable, and, when a trifling accident happens, or a little smoke gets in, all is confusion and bewilderment. Such places must always be considered dangerous. Stowage, improper, danger of.

The number and variety of stocks now found in great cities are such that no general rules can be laid down which would be applicable to all, but any intelligent person can without much difficulty judge for himself as to the safety or danger of any particular building by observing whether the stock is so inflammable that if it were once ignited a fire would spread over the whole or only a part before help could be brought, and also whether the structure is of such a kind and such a strength as to be likely of itself to resist the fire partially or altogether, or failing this to afford places at which firemen with proper appliances would have a chance of being able to make a stand. Stock, variety of. Stock, inflammability of.

Where combustible, inflammable, or explosive liquids are stored, care must be taken that the quantities are limited to such as are not likely to cause danger, and free ventilation into the open air should be provided. Liquids, explosive, storing.

16. Quantity of Stock.

Whatever a stock may consist of, it is certain that if it be stowed within a building in such quantities as nearly to fill the building, it is much more likely to be totally destroyed in case of fire than if it were stowed in moderate quantities, owing to the impossibility of getting water on it where most required. Stock, quantity of

Overloading buildings, danger of.

Instances have even occurred in which bales of fibrous and other substances were so stowed as to allow in ordinary times and at the temperature of the atmosphere passage for men and barrows, but when subjected to the heat of a fire the bales have burst their bands and expanded to such an extent as not only to close up the passages but also to force out the walls.

It is of very great importance, therefore, to the safety of a building that the quantity of its contents should be reasonably moderate and not excessive.

There can, of course, be no rigid rule laid down on such a subject, but a knowledge of the general principle of not overcrowding a building with goods will conduce to a correct judgment as to the risk in any particular cases.

Access prevented by overstocking.

It is much to be feared that in many large warehouses the rule is to refuse nothing, and to endeavour to stow away somehow every consignment of goods which arrives, even after the building is reasonably full. It is impossible otherwise to account for the excessive quantities of stock so often found in warehouses—quantities so enormous, in fact, that they not only prevent all proper access in case of fire, but even interfere to a very considerable extent with the ordinary examination and sale of the goods.

Theatres, restrictions regarding number of persons admitted.

Public buildings, such as theatres and others destined to contain large numbers of persons, should be licensed for only as many as can be properly accommodated. Thus, for instance, a theatre should be licensed for only as many as could be seated, leaving all the passages and gangways free and unobstructed. The practice of admitting persons when every seat is full has a dangerous effect in two ways, first by placing in the building a load greater than it has been made to carry, and secondly by crowding the passages and gangways to such an extent that in the event of an alarm of fire many persons would be unable to escape quickly, and would almost certainly lose their lives.

Theatres, unnecessary crowding.

Theatres, over-crowding, danger of.

In all places for the storage of valuable property or for manufacture of any kind, it would be a good precaution to have each room marked or registered for the weight it could safely carry, and also for the bulk of the goods to be contained in it, as a limitation of the weight only would not suffice to prevent a warehouse being filled with stock of a light description to such an extent as to close or reduce the gangways, and thus make speedy access impossible.

Rooms registered to carry weight and bulk.

In theatres and other buildings in which large numbers of persons assemble it would be well to have every part legibly marked for the number to be allowed to occupy it.

The danger of theatres and other buildings in which large numbers of persons are closely packed together would be still further reduced by removing manufacturing operations and stores altogether from under the roof of the main building to however short a distance with an open space between, and in many other similar ways which cannot be fully described here, as the subject of protecting life in such places is a very large and comprehensive one, and, moreover, sufficiently important to require a special treatise at some future time.

17. Classification of Stock.

Stock, classification of.

When substances of various kinds are deposited in the same building, it is of great importance that they should be so classified as to reduce the risk of a fire spreading. Thus in the case of solids, highly inflammable materials should be placed on the top, less inflammable materials below these, and so on to the bottom, where the least inflammable goods should be stowed. This is, in fact, the converse of the arrangement in ordinary use for lighting fires, which consists of a layer of highly inflammable material such as paper or shavings below, a layer of less inflammable material, wood, in the middle, and a layer of coal on top. It is obvious that, if the coal were placed below and the shavings on top, it would be at all times most difficult and in many cases quite impossible to make the fire spread.

Classification not recognised.

It seems most extraordinary, but it is nevertheless the case, that there are at present existing in some of the most important cities in this country large buildings for the deposit of miscellaneous goods of enormous value, in which the principles here laid down are not practically recognised, and this notwithstanding the repeated warnings given by the instantaneous spread of fires.

Classifying goods, danger arising from not.

There is nothing in the whole experience of a fireman so disheartening or unsatisfactory as being called to a fire, within perhaps 50 or 100 yards of his station, and finding on his arrival that the whole building is in flames, if not virtually destroyed. This may happen in the case of a dwelling house or other premises of ordinary description and moderate size through an accident or a combination of accidental circumstances not involving serious blame to any one; but in the case of a warehouse or other large building for the deposit of valuable miscellaneous goods it may almost always be attributed to gross and culpable negligence in the classification of the stock.

Concerning the stowage of inflammable liquids, such as fat oils, mineral oils, spirits, &c., no precise regulations can be made without reference to local and other circumstances, but the general rule may be laid down that these substances, though of different qualities, are all dangerous, and should only be stowed in buildings specially constructed to contain them, with complete separation between the several classes of goods. Liquids, inflammable, buildings specially constructed for storing.

It is very much to be feared, in fact it is almost a certainty, that in many places for the deposit of miscellaneous goods consignments on their arrival are placed in what may be at the moment the most convenient spots without the smallest reference to or consideration of their properties for receiving, communicating, or themselves generating fire. Goods, improper stowage of.

In the storing of mineral oils or other substances which discharge dangerous and inflammable vapours, provision should always be made for free ventilation into the open air—a point of paramount importance as a precaution against explosion. Oils, mineral, storing. Ventilation, free, in buildings where mineral oil is stored.

The proper classification of stock in shops and other retail places of business is in most cases simply impossible, and it is on this account that such premises are so dangerous. Instances are found of shops containing several thousand different descriptions of goods packed together in the closest proximity without the smallest attempt at even method, much less classification.

---

18. Classification of Trades.

Trades, classification of.

Where several trades are carried on under the same roof either by the same or different persons, some precaution might be taken that no undue risk of fire should arise therefrom, and in towns some summary process might be established for treating an infraction of the rule as a nuisance to be promptly suppressed.

Trades, different, under one roof.

The carrying on together of several different trades under the same roof, whether by one or by several persons, appears a proceeding of such very doubtful advantage, while its risks are beyond any doubt, that it would most probably in many cases be an act of economy to the general public to put a stop to it altogether.

Again, there is the important question of the proper classification of trades in separate buildings or separate districts so as to obviate unnecessary risk. Thus, for instance, a row of soundly and appropriately built warehouses might be loaded with a stock of spirits or spirit oils, and another row at a distance might contain furnaces for burning coke or fusing metals, and both might be considered safe in their respective ways; whereas if the buildings were placed alternately for the two trades, that is to say, if one house were to contain spirit oil and the next a furnace and so on for the remainder, the result would be that the risk of a fire commencing would be enormously increased, and the probability of its spreading after its commencement would be almost taken out of the category of risks, and become instead a certainty.

---

19. Accessibility.

The question of accessibility is one necessarily connected very closely with the three points last considered, namely, the nature, quantity, and classification of the stock, but it is treated separately for the purpose of calling special attention to it, as there are frequently cases in which goods not of a particularly inflammable character, not in undue quantity, and not improperly classified, are, nevertheless, so packed as to prevent all access to them in case of fire. Access prevented by stowage of goods.

When there are firemen with proper appliances in the neighbourhood, it may be laid down as a rule that the safety of the stock is in direct proportion to its accessibility, and that when persons in charge of warehouses stow their goods in such a manner as to prevent immediate access to them, they deliberately place them beyond the reach of help in case of danger. Access, safety of stock in proportion to.

Accessibility may in many cases depend to a great extent on the means of exit, as it may frequently be impossible for any one to enter until others have left.

In buildings, therefore, destined to contain large

Exit, means of. numbers of persons it is very strongly recommended that a few spots be left at intervals in walls, doors, gates, or partitions so arranged that in the event of an alarm they could easily be broken through, and thus additional means of exit be provided for an excited crowd.

Access by the roof. It would also be desirable that there should be occasional weak spots at intervals in the roof at which in the event of a fire a whole wing or other portion might be disconnected without delay and thus saved from destruction.

Exit, means of, to be used in emergencies. Large buildings, especially those laden with heavy stocks, should invariably be provided with several openings for exit, not necessarily for frequent use, but for cases of emergency, such as the outbreak of a fire when some one or more out of the number might be available, whereas if there were only one, that one might be rendered useless by heat, smoke, or flame, or through being blocked by falling materials.

20. Business carried on.

Business. Wherever any manufacture is carried on there is necessarily a risk distinct and separate from all other risks, and in almost all cases greater than that of mere deposit or stowage. It is therefore much to be regretted that in many valuable warehouses containing property of almost fabulous amount, economy or supposed economy has led to the introduction of such processes as carpen- Fires, use of, in warehouses. tering, coopering, brazing, glueing on a large scale, and many others requiring the partial or constant use of fires.

Wherever this is the case, the whole risk, however slight in all other particulars, should invariably be considered on a par with that of the manufacture carried on.

The necessities of commerce no doubt occasionally require that manufacturing operations should be carried on in the same buildings in which large quantities of valuable goods are stowed, but it cannot be too strongly impressed on those interested, that there is extreme danger in such a combination, and that, wherever it is found possible, the risks of deposit and manufacture should always be kept separate. Trades in warehouses, danger of carrying on.

The introduction of steam power of late years into almost every kind of business, and even in certain cases into private houses, while attended in some ways with many and great advantages, has undoubtedly increased the risk of fire to a very serious extent, and that in a fourfold manner, viz.— Steam-power in buildings.

Firstly, by causing direct danger of fire from the furnaces. Steam-power, danger to be apprehended by using.

Secondly, by friction.

Thirdly, by heating and desiccating buildings to such an extent that they are more easily set fire to, and burn more rapidly than formerly.

Fourthly, because the vibration of machinery set in structures or bearings not originally designed for such work weakens and fractures the walls to so great a degree that any additional concussion, such as occurs at fires by the falling in of a roof or floor, is likely to bring the whole building down, and so greatly increase the ultimate loss.

These are great and constantly increasing dangers.

Ranges, close-cooking. Another danger very frequently found is that resulting from the use of close-cooking ranges on the large scale now so common in eating houses, great warehouses, and other places. These stoves give out an enormous heat, and are usually connected with old flues, having only four inches of brickwork round them. The walls surrounding the ranges, or furnaces, as they might be called, become so heated that it is in many cases impossible to bear the hand on them, and all the adjoining woodwork becomes in course of time converted into a species of tinder, which blazes up to an enormous extent on the application of a spark.

Even where dangerous work is carried on, as, for instance, in theatres and other places of public amusement, much can be done for safety which will be found explained in Chapter 10, On Internal Divisions.

21. Heating.

Heating, artificial, danger of. There are dangers attending every kind of artificial heating, but they differ considerably in degree. In rooms properly ventilated and not containing spirits

Fireplaces, open. or other volatile liquids open fireplaces with screens in front to catch sparks may with ordinary supervision

Steam pipes. be used; steam pipes are always more or less objectionable on account of the danger of a leak from excessive pressure, and the consequent overheat of

Hot-water pipes. those parts next the furnace; hot water pipes properly laid on iron in brick or stone troughs made with cement, and not coming in contact with wood, with proper arrangements for supply, with a good circulation and with a safety valve in order, may be used without much risk; but the least dangerous mode of all is to heat air in a separate building and to pump or force it in at the required temperature. Hot air.

Such are the modes in common use, and although with proper precautions some of them may be adopted without much apprehension, still it is of importance to remember what has been already stated, namely, that there is some danger attending any artificial operation which raises the temperature of a building, or of the stock which it contains, above that of the surrounding atmosphere. Temperature.

Where stoves are used, great care must be taken to avoid the common and dangerous error of allowing them to stand on plates of iron laid on wood. In cases where stoves must be placed over floors, as, for instance, in the cabins of ships, the plates should be raised by an incombustible and non-conducting substance to a height of at least three inches above the woodwork, as to allow a free current of air to pass between, and even then the stoves ought to be very carefully watched to prevent overheat. Stoves, use of. Stoves, setting.

An iron stove plate laid on the floor causes wood or any other combustible material underneath it to become gradually charred, and finally to burst into a flame, before any danger is apprehended. Stove-plates, iron.

Many fires are caused by the improper setting of stoves and fireplaces.

Hot-water or steam pipes should on no account be allowed to rest on or touch timber in any part.

Stoves, close. Close stoves are almost invariably dangerous, as through neglect or ignorance on the part of those entrusted with their care they are likely to become red-hot in a very short time.

Fires, danger of drawing, on the hearth. The common practice of drawing a fire from the grate and dropping it on the hearthstone is dangerous, as the stone is not capable of resisting great heat. Fires allowed to burn out. It is generally much safer to allow the fire to burn out in the grate which is made for the purpose, or if for economy or any other reason it has to be drawn, care must be taken to watch the ashes until they are perfectly cool, and, where time is of importance to Ashes to be wetted. the care-taker, the ashes should be wetted. Heavy losses frequently happen through neglect of this simple precaution.

Air, burning. Any artificial heating which burns the air is most injurious to wood and all combustible materials, and renders them much more inflammable than they would be if only exposed to the temperature of the atmosphere.

---

22. Lighting.

Lighting, danger of. On the subject of lighting the same may be said in general terms as on that of heating, namely, that there is danger in all artificial means employed for the purpose.

Two points are especially to be observed; first, that where there is light there is an increase of temperature; the other, that where there is light there is flame.

Wherever there is artificial light there should invariably be abundant ventilation, by which term is meant, not merely a good supply of fresh air or merely a free discharge of foul air, but a proper combination of these two requisites; in short, to use an objectionable but expressive word, a draught. Ventilation.

When the heat is much concentrated it makes substances highly inflammable which might at a low temperature be simply combustible; and when the flame is much concentrated it is likely to become unmanageable, and to extend to all combustible substances near it. Heat and flame concentrated.

The light of, say, a thousand candles, if distributed in small fragments over such a space as would commonly be occupied by a thousand candlesticks, might be comparatively safe, whereas the same amount of light, collected as closely together as it sometimes is by coiled, circular, or other gas pipes, might be full of danger, producing as it does sufficient heat not only for warming ovens, or cooking on a gigantic scale, but even for fusing metals.

On this account light should never be concentrated on a large scale except under the advice of experienced persons, and in buildings specially prepared for the purpose.

The least dangerous of all modes of artificial lighting would be to have lanterns in the wall with only external ventilation, and a system of reflectors inside to distribute the light wherever it might be required. This plan has been successfully adopted in many large and valuable warehouses. Lanterns placed in walls.

A safe mode of supplying small quantities of light in dangerous premises is by oil lamps, which after Oil lamps in dangerous premises.

being lighted in a separate place and then locked can be placed on slate brackets distributed throughout the building for that purpose, and in the event of any being extinguished they could not be lighted by the watchman or others, but must be brought back to the lamp-room and others issued in their stead.

Gas may be a less expensive mode of lighting, but it is attended by so many risks that in certain buildings it ought not to be used at all.

Lamp, shed, detached.

Even the mode of lighting here pointed out with its, perhaps, troublesome restrictions, though less dangerous than many others, cannot in some valuable warehouses be put in operation without the strictest supervision, and the lamps should not be trimmed or prepared for use in any part of the main building, but a shed of non-combustible material should be provided outside for this purpose, as the cotton waste used for cleaning when saturated with oil is liable to what is commonly known as spontaneous ignition.

Gas brackets, swinging, and shades, swinging.

Where gas brackets are used they should not be allowed so much swing as to reach woodwork or curtains, and if they are guarded by swinging *not fixed* shades above, there should be no particular cause for anxiety from this cause.

Gas-jets, metal cages for.

Where curtains, blinds, or other light articles are in close proximity as to incur a probability of being blown on the gas jets, the latter should be covered with wire cages or other metal guards.

These guards are themselves, however, a source of danger unless made of sufficient size to prevent direct contact of the flame with any substance falling on them. In practice it is found that a guard of this kind ought not to be within three inches of any part of the flame, as light substances will readily ignite at that distance; and where it is inconvenient to have cages of this size, it is much better to have none at all, as in this latter case there may be a probability of the light being extinguished by the material coming in contact with it.

With regard to the use of gas it should be mentioned that the common mode of turning off all the lights at the meter is not good, as it involves the necessity of some responsible person going round to turn off *every* cock before it is safe to turn on the gas at the meter again, and it is hardly to be supposed that this can always be done with the necessary precision. It is much safer never to turn the gas off at the meter, as it is better to let gas burn away than to allow it to escape into the air and mix in such proportions as to cause a liability to explosion. Perhaps this latter danger may be better understood when it is mentioned that if a small room or other enclosed space be filled with a mixture of gas and air in the proportion of one volume of gas to six of air, it would, on contact with a mere spark, explode with a violence sufficient to blow up a whole building. Gas, turning off.

Where gas is used in large quantities, as in mansions, theatres, and places of public entertainment, warehouses, &c., it should invariably be under the immediate and direct control of a competent practical man. Gas under control of competent person.

The enormous heat in the roofs of theatres and other places of entertainment during the performances is so great that all the woodwork becomes desiccated and converted into something like touchwood, and can be ignited by a mere spark.

Gas pipes, visible.

It would be a great advantage in all buildings lighted with gas to have the pipes visible throughout, and not, as they commonly are, imbedded in the walls.

Gas pipes, material for.

As a rule, all gas pipes should be of hard metal. Instances are frequent in which every soft pipe in a house is melted during the early stages of a fire, and the gas escapes and adds considerably to the danger both of fire and explosion, while the iron or other hard metal pipes are generally quite uninjured, as they cannot be destroyed or even weakened except by very intense heat.

Command cocks.

Meter, position of.

Every building lighted with gas should have two command cocks to the main pipe, one inside and the other outside the house; and where there is a meter, it should be placed in such a position as to have free ventilation into the open air.

Gas, combustion of.

Gas jets, glass chimneys for.

The combustion of gas is much more complete, and consequently the danger of unconsumed or partly consumed gas escaping is much diminished, if every jet is mounted with a glass chimney. Safety in this way is also further secured by mounting over the top of the glass chimney, but not touching it, a small piece of talc or metal, which helps to cause a complete consumption of the gas.

Gas jets, distance of, from ceiling.

Shades, swinging.

Gas jets should not be placed nearer than thirty-six inches from the ceiling over, and argand burners or other concentrated lights should not be nearer than forty-eight inches, and all gas brackets should be fitted on the sides with stops to prevent them travelling beyond a safe distance and on the top with swinging (not fixed) shades, which by keeping up a light motion serve to distribute the heat.

Even the introduction of natural light inside a building is sometimes not without its risks. Thus, for instance, bow windows in rows or streets are dangerous, as they are liable to communicate fire from one house to another. Well holes also, with windows in the middle of a house, are dangerous if the windows are in more than one side of the well, as they are liable to communicate fire from one window to another.

Windows, bow.

Windows, well-hole.

Iron shutters or screens on the high windows of large buildings should be so fitted as to be capable of being opened on an emergency from the outside. Many valuable buildings have been destroyed by fire through the absence of this precaution. Where iron shutters are used they should be fitted with handles in such a way that they could be opened either from the outside or the inside on all the levels above the first floor. Heavy losses have resulted through the firemen being unable to open shutters from the outside after they had been expanded by the heat.

Iron shutters opening outside.

Glass used for glazing should be free from bull's-eyes or dents, especially where exposed to the direct rays of the sun. Many losses of property have been caused by the rays of the sun becoming concentrated in this way and setting fire to buildings.

Windows, glass for.

23. Special Risks.

Separate risks.

In the present condition of commerce no survey can be considered complete which does not include a clear and precise entry on the subject of special risks; that is to say, an entry stating whether there are or are not any risks of a class distinct and separate from those of the ordinary trade ostensibly carried on.

Thus, for instance, there may be two premises of about the same size, build, and shape, both known as warehouses for the storage of the same description of goods, containing about equal stocks, and to an ordinary observer both presenting the same appearance externally and internally, and yet a careful professional survey might bring to light that, while one transacted only its proper, legitimate, or ostensible business, the other added some operation involving the use of a

Use of steam-engine on premises.

steam engine and furnaces, with as a consequence a large storage of coal, wood, shavings, and other

Stowing inflammable material.

inflammable materials on the premises; in other words the professional survey might show that, while one building was comparatively safe, the other might be in the utmost possible danger; or, to use our simple technical language, while one was an ordinary risk, the other might be extra hazardous.

In making a survey, therefore, it is of great importance to observe this point with extreme accuracy, and to make a special entry concerning it.

Points of danger.

There are several points of danger common to many warehouses and other buildings containing valuable property.

1. Packing and unpacking goods.
2. Furnaces for working machinery.
3. Cooking.
4. Waste and oil for cleaning machinery.
5. Dust heaps.
6. Shavings and sawdust.
7. Felt roofs.
8. Other sources.

Packing and unpacking.

This in many large warehouses and other places of business is generally the first and greatest danger, and must be carefully watched. During the operation of either packing or unpacking there is commonly an enormous quantity of hay, straw, paper, and other inflammable substances, loose about the premises, and the workmen and carriers should be searched for matches or pipes recently smoked, which they frequently put in their pockets without properly extinguishing them. Packing and unpacking. Loose hay and straw. Workmen searched for pipes.

As soon as goods are unpacked, the carriers should remove the cases, wrappers, and other lumber, which should, if possible, not be stored either in the main building or in any shed or other structure adjoining. Storing empty cases.

Clearing away rubbish. While packing and unpacking are going on, there should be persons constantly employed in sweeping up and removing all rubbish which is found on, or under, or in the crevices of the flooring, and clear passages should always be kept at each side for firemen and others to pass in case of need.

Furnaces for working machinery.

Furnaces in detached buildings. Furnaces required for working machinery should, if possible, be placed in buildings constructed of incombustible materials and at a safe distance from the nearest parts of buildings containing valuable property. Consuming smoke. These furnaces should consume their own smoke, as otherwise there is but little protection from top sparks, inasmuch as the ordinary gratings stop the draught considerably, and, if they do not wear out, the workmen frequently remove then to increase the draught. Storing fuel. The fuel for furnaces should not be stored in any shed or other structure in communication with the main building.

Cooking.

Cooking in separate building. Where cooking is required it should be done, if possible, in a separate building, and no fire for this purpose, whether of spirits, gas, coal, coke, or any other substance or material, should on any account be permitted within a warehouse or other building containing large quantities of valuable property.

Waste and oil for cleaning machinery.

In buildings containing machinery there are many appliances requiring constant cleaning and oiling, and consequently the presence of waste and oil frequently scattered about in somewhat large quantities. Where such is the case a rule should be made that persons using cotton rags, waste, or oil, should have a safe tin or iron box to hold the same, as these substances are liable to spontaneous ignition, and if neglected may constitute an element of very serious danger.

Buildings containing machinery.

Use of oily waste.

Dust heaps.

Dust should not be permitted to accumulate in heaps either on or under the flooring, but should be carefully swept up, removed outside, and carted away as often as necessary.

Dust, removal of.

Shavings and sawdust.

In places where carpentering or any similar process is carried on great care should be taken to prevent accumulations of shavings or sawdust either on or under the floors, and persons employed in removing the dust should pay strict attention to this point also, which is advisedly entered in a separate paragraph in order that it may attract special attention.

Shavings, removal of.

Felt roofs.

Roofs, felt danger of.

Temporary structures are frequently covered in with felt instead of slates, but this material is generally very dangerous.

During the heat of spring and summer the felt and all the adjoining woodwork attain so high a temperature that the slightest spark falling on them may cause them to blaze up instantly.

Roofs, felt, cooling.

This requires close watching, and wherever it is used there should be external hydrants always available for cooling the roof and the outside generally during very hot weather.

Some responsible person, as, for instance, the principal fireman, if there be one, should have charge of this very important matter, and the cooling of the roof and walls outside would be no inconvenience, but, on the contrary, a source of comfort to persons inside.

Roofs, felt, protection or.

A thin sprinkling of sand may with advantage be scattered over the felt, and woollen coverings might be kept in readiness, which would prove a considerable protection during the hot days of summer, and when wetted would be a complete safeguard against the great heat.

Other sources of danger.

Lightning.

Other sources of danger which should be provided for are *lightning*, which, if the building be not of itself a lightning conductor, as it ought to be, may be easily guarded against by copper rods twenty feet above the roof and running into the ground at intervals of about 100 feet; *malicious burning*, the probability of which can only be calculated by local information; and what is commonly known as *spontaneous ignition*, which may be guarded against by the use of the iron boxes already mentioned and by constant cleanliness and ventilation being strictly enforced in every part of the premises. Incendiarism. Spontaneous ignition.

Smoking, artificial heating, and the carrying on of dangerous processes requiring the use of fires, are, as a general rule, utterly inadmissible in light temporary buildings. In such structures, when it is absolutely necessary that some artificial heat should be provided during the cold seasons of the year, the least dangerous method of heating would be to have a few open fireplaces with a careful man in charge of each, but in very light buildings even with this precaution there would be considerable danger, which, if at all possible, should be avoided. Smoking. Fireplaces, open.

Close stoves are always dangerous, as they are liable at any moment to become red-hot furnaces and to set fire to everything near them. Stoves, close.

It is very desirable to prevent as far as possible the erection of sheds or tents in the immediate vicinity of a building containing valuable property, and, where these are absolutely necessary, they should be constructed of non-combustible materials, and should be under the control of, and constantly visited by, some responsible persons. Sheds and tents, erection of.

Erections of this kind should on no account be in direct communication with the main building.

In many places steam-vessels of various sizes are in the habit of lighting fires before starting, and drawing Steam-vessels alongside wharves.

them after returning, in close proximity to valuable wharves and warehouses.

This is a highly dangerous practice, and should on no account be permitted.

No valuable wharf or waterside premises can be considered safe in which there is not a stringent rule, that steam-vessels shall not light or draw fires when alongside them, but that they must haul out into the stream for that purpose.

Chimneys, smoke-consuming.

The chimneys of all boilers and furnaces in towns or in the proximity of other premises should be made to consume their own smoke, or failing this should be mounted with screens or gratings to intercept sparks and ashes, and so prevent them being blown on other buildings and thus causing fires.

Lumber stowing.

The practice of piling spare furniture and other lumber in basements is most dangerous and should be avoided, and that of allowing carpentering and other work to be done in such places with families or property over them is wholly incompatible with safety.

Ash pits.

Buildings of all kinds, whether used as residences, factories, warehouses, or for any other purposes, should be provided with strong well-placed ash-pits, constructed of brick or some other incombustible material.

24. Surrounding and External Risks.

It frequently happens that a building comparatively safe in itself may be in danger from some of those surrounding or adjoining.

Thus, to take a possibility, a building may be constructed throughout of incombustible materials, and contain nothing but a stock of metal, thus being in itself perfectly safe, and yet the fact of a gunpowder manufactory adjoining might place it in imminent danger of destruction by explosion; or, to take a less extreme case, a high warehouse containing inflammable goods, but well watched and with very slight danger from internal causes, may have a number of windows overlooking a low building in which a highly dangerous trade is carried on, and may consequently, though almost safe in itself, be in the utmost danger in case of a fire happening in the adjoining premises. **Buildings, safe and unsafe, in close proximity.**

A careful survey should therefore be made of all the surroundings, in order to ascertain how far a building is in the risk of others.

It is highly advisable that steamers should be prohibited not only from lighting or drawing their fires, but also from working their hoisting engines alongside or in the immediate proximity of warehoures, but where this is done the danger is much reduced by having the funnels covered on the top with screens to intercept the sparks. **Steamers alongside warehouses.**

The stowage of goods outside premises, as, for instance, on footways in front of shops, or on piers or wharves alongside warehouses, is always dangerous. **Stowage of goods outside warehouses.**

25. Watching.

Buildings, watching.

It is essential to the safety of every large building containing a heavy or valuable stock that it should be well watched, so that any fire happening in it should be immediately discovered, and it is generally advisable that the watch should have at command some means of quickly suppressing a fire.

In large cities it is too much the practice to trust all buildings by night to the general care of the patrolling police, many of whom have beats which even in ordinary times occupy them at least twenty or thirty minutes to go round, and in cases of detention, which from various causes must happen several times every night, involve occasional absences of some forty or fifty minutes duration from any given spot.

Buildings, special watching of.

It is therefore plain that something more is necessary to secure even comparative safety, and it may be laid down as a rule that any building of exceptional size or value, or requiring exceptional care, should have a special watch, and that any building of such a character without this precaution should be considered dangerous.

Watchmen, access to all parts of building.

On general principles any man employed on such a duty as that of watching valuable premises should be a trustworthy person, and, being so, he should be entrusted with the keys of the premises, and have access to every part. Unfortunately, however, it is impossible in the practical working of commerce on the gigantic scale now so common to allow any one uncontrolled access to the goods, and the result is that many very valuable buildings, even when provided with a so-called watchman, are very imperfectly watched.

Again, the fear which owners of valuable property Te have of their watchmen falling asleep is occasionally so cl great as to lead them to establish on their premises what are known as tell-tale clocks. On these clocks the watchmen record their rounds, if they make them at the proper time, by pushing in pegs, but at any other time they cannot do so, and the masters, when they come in the morning, can by looking at the clocks ascertain whether the watchmen have gone all their rounds correctly.

These machines are very simple and to a certain class of minds may appear very effective, but their adoption is founded on an utterly wrong principle, namely, that of distrusting confidential servants, and consequently their use is not to be practically relied on beyond a very limited extent.

Instances are on record in which fires have occurred in close proximity to large and valuable buildings provided with watchmen, and yet no alarm has been given by the watchmen, as, although they had great suspicions, they were obliged to leave the points where danger was apprehended and go to other parts of the buildings to attend to the duties assigned to them of pegging their clocks.

An instance also is on record in which a building standing in its own grounds was watched by four men, two of whom patrolled within and two without the walls, and yet the alarm of a fire which happened in this building was first given by a street constable, who happened to see the light while going round his beat. If there had been but one watchman, or even two, might have been possible to impute some blame to them, but, as there were four, it was much more reasonable to assume that they were engaged in pegging clocks or carrying out some other so-called self-registering scheme of recording their duties instead of really transacting them.

Watchmen not having free access. In cases where watchmen are kept who are not allowed complete access to every part of the premises, it is advisable, wherever possible, to provide points of observation by inserting bull's-eyes or other thick pieces of glass in such places as command a view over the premises.

Watchmen employed externally. Watchmen employed only externally, or with very limited access or none at all to the inside parts containing much bulk of property, may possibly be of use for keeping thieves away and for other purposes, but they can be of very little service either for discovering a fire or for stopping it when discovered.

In short, the safety of a building consists to a very great extent in the manner in which it is watched, and watching can be considered really effective only when it is carried on freely and completely and without restrictions.

All these points must be carefully considered in any complete inspection of a building for the purpose of ascertaining its risk, and special reference made to them in the report on the survey.

26. Water Supply.

The danger of a building through fire is very much reduced when there is an abundant supply of water on the premises, with good distributing pipes and proper means of projection. Water supply.

There are many ways of supplying water for extinguishing fire, and of these the best and safest is to have a tower on or adjoining the premises, with a tank at a height of about thirty feet above the roof, but this is a most expensive arrangement, and is consequently not very frequently adopted. The next best way is to take the water from external pipes constantly kept under such a pressure that the water can be thrown with force to the highest parts of the building. Water supply from roof. Water supply, external.

With either of these arrangements there should be within the building distributing pipes mounted with proper hydrants so close to each other as not to require more than about forty or fifty feet of hose or flexible pipe to reach any part of the premises, that being as large a quantity as can be rapidly handled by one or two men. The mode of distribution must in every case depend on the general plan and construction of the premises, but it should always consist of at least one vertical pipe the whole height of the premises, and as many horizontal pipes throughout the several floors as are required for mounting the necessary number of hydrants—that is to say, such a number as to ensure that there shall be no spot which cannot be reached by about forty or fifty feet of hose. Distributing pipes. Mode of distribution. Hydrants.

The next best way is to have external pipes under Constant pressure.

Hydrants in streets.

constant pressure, with hydrants or other means of access to the water, in convenient parts of the streets. The difference between this mode and that last pointed out is that in this the quantity of hose required to reach high or distant parts of the premises is considerable, and the loss of time in laying it out and getting the water through it is proportionately great.

Ponds, canals, &c.

The next best way is to have an abundance of water in a pond, canal, river, or other large open receptacle in close proximity to the premises, with proper means at command for forcing it wherever it may be required.

Intermittent pressure.

The least satisfactory mode of all, and that which in many towns is unfortunately the most common, is to have external pipes with intermittent and generally very uncertain pressure.

This arrangement has many drawbacks, the two principal of which are, first, that at best the supply must necessarily be very limited in comparison with that obtained from rivers or open reservoirs; and secondly, that it is likely to deceive the inmates, by giving them a sense of security which in reality has very little foundation, and thus, perhaps, leading them to incur risks which in the absence of this false sense of security they would make every effort to avoid.

Water arrangements in large buildings.

Of the ignorance occasionally displayed in the water arrangements of valuable premises it is impossible to speak too severely. There are cases in which tanks are placed either on or under a roof, and distributing pipes of the most approved kind mounted with the best hydrants, leading all over the premises, and, no doubt, he owners, after going to so much expense, believe that everything has been done to secure the immediate suppression of fires at their commencement, whereas any professional fireman would see at a glance that the pipes would at best be available only for the lower levels; that on the upper floors the pressure of water would not be sufficient to open ordinary leather hose and force its way through, and that under no circumstances whatever could the water be made available for anything which might happen on or immediately under the roof. Instances have even occurred where large sums have been expended in providing rising mains, horizontal distributing pipes, hose, and all other necessary appliances, and yet where it has been entirely forgotten or neglected to connect the internal pipes with the external main from which alone the supply could be obtained, and the owners or managers, after years of false confidence, have been made aware of the omission only on the occurrence of the very casualty for which they had previously supposed themselves to be so well prepared.

Water-arrangements defective.

Again, it is not unusual in buildings with an abundant supply of water under constant and ample pressure and with good distributing pipes mounted with a sufficient number of hydrants or fire-cocks, to find some of the appliances or gear of so bad a pattern as to reduce the means of delivering water very considerably below what they seem to be. For instance, to take the most common case of all, it is frequently found that hydrants or stand-pipes, and sometimes even couplings, fitted with what are commonly known as $2\frac{1}{2}$ inch screws, instead of having a clear circular passage of $2\frac{1}{2}$ inches in diameter, are throttled somewhere inside to a diameter of $1\frac{1}{2}$ inches, thus leaving the real water-way

Fire appliances, defective.

very little more than a third of the proper area, while the weight for moving about and the expense in providing are in no way diminished.

These are most important points for consideration in making a survey.

Intermittent supply.

With an intermittent supply of water the dependence of those entrusted with the safety of a building should be placed solely on the pumping power of engines, as the pressure from a main when first turned on cannot be safely relied on to deliver water in the high parts of a building.

Rising mains mounted with hydrants.

In buildings likely to be filled with crowds of persons it is not enough to have hydrants only on the ground level. Rising mains or service pipes should be continued up to the roof, galleries, or other high levels, and should be mounted with hydrants for hose and with common cocks for filling buckets.

Cisterns.

There should also be provided in the high levels a number of cisterns, and it is an advantage, wherever possible, to have some of these in the galleries and some on the roof.

Cisterns, filling.

These cisterns need not necessarily be in connection with the mains, as they could be filled by hose from the nearest hydrant.

Crowded buildings.

If there were to be no visitors in a building at the breaking out of a fire, hydrants without cisterns might perhaps be sufficient for all purposes; but, as it would be clearly impossible for firemen or others entrusted with the safety of the place to carry up their hose and other gear into the galleries through a dense crowd, excited and bewildered as they (*the crowd*) would be during the first moments of an alarm, it is most desirable to have both hydrants and cisterns in the galleries, roofs, and other high levels of buildings containing large numbers of persons.

Fire-engines are portable machines for pumping water already provided, and they are effective, not only in accordance with the power which can be applied by their means, but also in proportion to the time which they take to get to work. It is no part of their function to provide water from great depths or long distances, although, unfortunately, they have frequently to be used for this purpose. So little attention has been paid to this point that instances are found in which large and valuable warehouses, though almost completely surrounded by water, are absolutely unprovided with any means of making the water available for the use of fire-engines until after a loss of time which must in many cases be fatal to success.

It is therefore a matter of paramount importance in a survey to ascertain with precision the time which a fire-engine will occupy in removing water from the place in which it is provided to the spot at which it is required, and any survey which omits precise information on this essential point must be considered untrustworthy and bad.

27. Fire-Engines, Hose, and other Appliances.

Fire-engines, &c.

Fire appliances, moveable. Where there is a water supply on a tower over a building, and a proper system of distributing pipes, there is still required a stock of hose, branches, nozzles, spanners, and other articles, in order to obtain access to the water and partly to convey, partly to project, it to any point at which it may be required. For the selection and preparation of these appliances no particular instructions can be given which would be applicable to all cases, but the general principle may be laid down, that the moveable gear should be in accordance with the size of the pipes, the pressure of the water on them, and the circumstances of the place.

Hydrants, size of. Thus, for instance, if there be an independent water tower for the sole use of the premises, with a tank at a height of 100 feet above the roof, and distributing service pipes of not less than 4 inches in diameter in any part, the hydrants may safely be mounted with outlets of $2\frac{1}{2}$ inches in diameter, the hose may have a $2\frac{1}{2}$ inch water-way, and the ordinary working nozzle may be fully 1 inch in diameter; whereas if the tank be only 40 or 50 feet above the roof, and the services only 2 inches in diameter, it will be found preferable Size of hose and nozzles. to use $1\frac{1}{2}$ inch hose with nozzles of only $\frac{1}{2}$ an inch, or one fourth of the area used with the higher tanks and larger pipes.

Unequal pressure of water on external pipes.

Again, for a water supply, not independent as from a tower, but obtained from external pipes with varying pressure caused by the varying requirements of other places, it is well to calculate the sizes and forms of all the appliances in such a way that they may be suitable to the supply when at its worst or weakest. Thus, for instance, when the pressure on the external pipes varies from 100 lbs. on each square inch, which is equivalent to that of a column of water 230 feet high, to 30 lbs. which corresponds with that of a column under 70 feet high, all the arrangements should be made for delivering the water under the lower pressure, and the pipes and moveable gear should be made much smaller and lighter than would be necessary for obtaining the full advantage of the higher column, as the water with only a pressure of 30 lbs. on each square inch might be unable to open the heavy hose necessary for withstanding a pressure of 100 lbs. on the square inch and the nozzle most effective with the high pressure, might not deliver the water more than a few feet from the orifice under the lower service.

Many valuable buildings have been lost through neglect or ignorance of these points.

Engines employed to lift water.

Where there is no pressure either from a high tank or external pipes it is necessary to have an engine to force the water up, and this can be either fixed or moveable, according to circumstances. For instance, if there be a pond, river, or reservoir close to the premises, a pipe may be led from it with a rising main and distributing services all over the building, and a fixed engine may be mounted over the pipe at some convenient spot outside, clear of all danger from falling walls, &c., and this engine may be worked, when required, so as to force the water up with a pressure only limited by the strength of the men or other power employed. The same work can be done, but less perfectly, by an engine with its suction pipe in the reservoir, and its delivery pipe attached to the rising main or distributing services.

Hose.

In cases where there is no water service under pressure, and where there are no fixed distributing pipes, it is necessary to have an engine with flexible hose of sufficient length to reach from where the water is supplied to every part of the premises, and of such weight and handiness as to suit the convenience of the persons who would have to use it.

Competent man in charge of engine.

When engines are required to pump the water up, it is found often necessary and always advisable to have in charge of them men thoroughly conversant with their construction and use, and capable of setting right mistakes, and working the machine under all circumstances.

Engines are frequently found in valuable premises in perfectly good order, and yet absolutely unfit for work in the hands of unskilled persons, merely because a simple cock is turned in one direction instead of another, or because a nut is slack, or a joint not properly hardened up.

All these points must be carefully included in the inspection of a building.

Portable Apparatus.

The portable appliances, as far as they can be enumerated, should generally be all or several of the following articles, namely:

Engines. Fire appliances portable.

Standpipes.

Buckets.

Hose in lengths of 40 or 50 feet each.

Hose Reels.

Hand-pumps with pails.

Hand-pumps without pails.

A proportion of tools distributed throughout.

One size and pattern of screws should invariably be adopted over the whole of a building and for the engines, hose, standpipes, &c., and the threads of the screws should be round, not V-shaped. Screws, uniform.

Branches or directing pipes should on no account be more than 18 inches long, including the nozzles. Branches, length of.

Fire-pumps or, as they are more commonly called, hand-pumps, should be provided for houses and offices containing valuable property. These little machines are very simple and can be worked by any one. Being made rather ornamental, they can be kept in prominent places in the corridors or passages, and will be found exceedingly useful for stopping a fire at an early stage. Hand-pumps.

The other articles are very simple and need not be separately described.

28. External Means of Protection.

External protection. The safety of a building consists, among many other matters, to a great extent on the means which may be at hand for suppressing a fire immediately on its occurrence, not only within the premises, but also in the vicinity, and consequently an inspection or survey, to be complete, should invariably extend to all the surroundings for the purpose of ascertaining the external means of protection.

In towns the ostensible means can easily be ascertained, but these should in no case be absolutely relied on until the person making the inspection has ascertained for himself that they are as they are represented to be, as it is a certain fact, however much to be surprised at or regretted, that there are many cities in the world, and still more towns, which, though they pay some attention to their fire appliances, and incur some expenditure on them, are nevertheless practically without means of protection, owing in most cases to an utter absence of organization, and in many to an absence of a proper controlling head, capable of taking the lead and directing others in an emergency. Cases are even to be found where the inhabitants of a town spend vast sums on their fire appliances, and are very proud and boastful of them, and yet where a real fireman would condemn the stock as useless and the staff as absolutely ignorant of almost everything connected with the profession.

Organization.

Head of brigade.

Again, there are instances in which buildings are well-constructed, not improperly loaded, and in the immediate neighbourhood of powerful aid from without, and yet these buildings are liable to be destroyed by any fire, however small at the commencement, owing to the inaccessibility of the premises, either in consequence of the approaches being too narrow or altogether obstructed. Inaccessibility of premises.

---

29. General Remarks.

There are again other matters not connected with the subject of construction, or very specially with any of the points previously mentioned, but rather with the domestic arrangements and daily work of a house, which should receive some notice here, namely, the position of the store-rooms, which are often found in the hottest parts of a house, perhaps over a kitchen,—that of carpenters' shops in basements containing in many cases most unnecessary quantities of timber, the use of oil lamps the heat of which passes up through flues thick with lampblack, &c. Domestic arrangements. Store-rooms, position of. Oil lamps, use of.

These things may in many places have existed for a long time without causing danger, but it would be ignoring all practical experience not to state plainly that their continuance is wholly incompatible with the safety of buildings.

Thorough ventilation is generally an excellent preventive of fires, but, after a fire has once commenced, only as much air should be admitted as may be necessary for respiration. Ventilation

Dustbins or heaps should be placed outside buildings, and have free ventilation into the open air, as Dustbins, construction of.

their contents are liable to fermentation or spontaneous ignition, and, moreover, occasionally become the receptacles for hot ashes, or even lighted cinders. The bins should be constructed of brick or some other fireproof materials.

Lightning conductors. Every building should be provided with a lightning conductor.

The following precautions are recommended, namely—

Deposit of animal or vegetable matter. All places in which are deposited animal or vegetable matter should be thoroughly ventilated with dry air, constantly watched, and frequently cleared out.

Lumber-rooms. Lumber rooms should be outside buildings, not inside.

Danger in large buildings. It must be kept in mind that many valuable buildings in their materials, mode of construction, and enormous cubic dimensions contain the greatest known elements of danger from fire, and very often not one element of safety, such as a party wall or other point at which the firemen or others entrusted with their protection would have reasonable hope of even temporarily retarding the progress of a large fire.

In such buildings every precaution should be taken to stop a fire at its first commencement, as under unfavorable circumstances it can never be stopped at any other stage.

Safety of buildings. After entering fully into an enumeration of the dangers of a building, attention should be called to its points of safety, where they exist, such as, for instance, the excellence and soundness of arches and lower parts of the structure generally, its comparatively moderate height, and its accessibility in every part both inside and out. The latter point is of so great importance that in a building accessible from all points it may be considered to be almost impossible for a fire to spread with such rapidity as to cause loss of life, unless under most exceptional circumstances.

It should be remembered that the safety of a building frequently depends as much on vigilance and prevention as on having such complete preparations that a fire may be extinguished immediately on its first discovery.

Once more, therefore, it is most strongly recommended that the best safeguards against fire are perfect ventilation, scrupulous cleanliness, complete preparations, and, above all, the best possible watching.

In order to make some of the views here set forward more intelligible, the following brief summary is added of facts which have taken place at recent dates, and which attracted much attention among persons interested in the protection of property from fire.

In the autumn of one year, and again in the beginning of the next, there were serious fires in some large waterside premises, and on both occasions large stocks of inflammable materials were stored in warehouses constructed of brick, wood, iron, and stone.

After each of these fires the following results were observed:—The bricks were uninjured, the wood was seriously damaged, but only partially consumed, the iron was fractured, and consequently rendered worthless, and the stone was shivered into fragments and totally destroyed. Re dis aft fir

At a fire which took place in the basement of a private house a cupboard and some small articles of furniture were burned, and the fire was confined to the spot in which it originated. The stairs leading from the basement to the ground floor were of stone, and were separated from the basement by a door and partition, both of wood, only half an inch thick in the panels, and this door and partition, though very much charred on the inside and blistered by the heat on the outside, were not burned through. No fire whatever reached the stone stairs, and nothing but heat either from above or below; no water was thrown on them to cool them suddenly, and no draught of cold air from outside passed over them; and yet they were broken into fragments and totally destroyed up as far as the first landing, where they ended, and the wooden stairs commenced.

Stone staircase, destruction of.

At a fire which took place in a private house, and which resulted in the loss of two lives, a stone stairs which reached from the basement to the landing on the third floor was totally destroyed, scarcely a vestige remaining in the well hole to show what material the steps had been composed of. In this case the heat which affected the stone was caused by the burning of the kitchen furniture and of the doors on the several landings. The fire communicated to the wooden landing on the third floor and the wooden stairs from that to the roof, two stories higher. It is needless to point out that under these circumstances the heat and flame must have been much more intense at the top of the well than at the bottom, and yet the draught of cold air caused by the opening of the front door brought the whole of the stone stairs down in a mass of fragments into the basement, leaving all the wooden parts on fire certainly, but still standing, and

Superiority of wood over stone.

so little injured that, when they were extinguished a few minutes afterwards, the firemen were able to walk about on them, and to do the whole of the remaining work from the inside of the building, having obtained access to the wooden landing on the third floor by means of the ordinary fire ladders.

At fires which took place in two very large public buildings the utter worthlessness of stone and iron for resisting even moderately high temperatures such as 600° or 700° Fahrenheit has been exemplified in a very instructive manner, and in both cases the comparative safety of wood and the absolute safety of bricks have been most strikingly illustrated.

At a fire which took place in some large warehouses all the stone stairs and the so-called fire-proof flooring failed utterly at an early stage, and as it was consequently impossible for the firemen to do their work inside, a large destruction of property took place, which certainly would *not* have been the case had there been means of access to the several floors either by wrought-iron stairs, strong enough to bear the weight of the men, but not so heavy as to be in danger of coming down with their own weight, or even by sound and well-constructed wooden stairs with wooden landings over.

A fire occurred in a house at the corner of two streets supported altogether by iron columns, and at an early stage of the fire the supports softened, and the house without a moment's warning fell completely down, not leaving a vestige of any kind, except a small portion of a chimney breast, to show where it had originally stood.

On this occasion two lives were lost.

Building erected on iron columns. There is at the present moment to be seen at the corner of two streets a new building recently erected, 90 feet long, 24 feet deep, and from 70 to 80 feet high, supported entirely on iron columns without any wall, wood, or brickwork, reaching to the ground along the whole line of the front. There is no doubt that at the ordinary temperature of from 600° to 700° Fahrenheit the whole building must inevitably fall down, and such a temperature could easily be created by the combustion of a very small quantity of household furniture or any other inflammable articles.

Efficiency of brigade. There cannot be the slightest doubt about the great good which can be effected by a thoroughly efficient fire brigade, but it is no less certain that, however perfect the supply and distribution of water, or the mechanical appliances and personal intrepidity and skill of a fire brigade may be, still the safety of any great city, and more particularly of any mercantile city containing a great amount of massed property, must eventually depend to a much greater degree than has hitherto been acknowledged on the mode in which its buildings are constructed and the property within them classified with special reference to risk of fire.

30. General Results of Survey.

After the foregoing subjects have been thus gone Re su
into separately, they should be considered as they bear on and affect each other, due prominence being given to the more important, and all being carefully weighed and balanced together; and the whole should conclude with a condensed summary assessing the risk as ordinary, hazardous, very hazardous, or otherwise, according to the judgment of the person making the survey.

INDEX.

A.

B.

C.

E.

F.

I.

L.

M.

T.

U.

V.

W.

EFFINGHAM WILSON, PRINTER, ROYAL EXCHANGE.